GULLIVER'S COLLECTIBLES

The Net User's Guide to Buying, Selling, and Trading Collectibles

R. J. Gulliver

Stoddart

Published in 2000 by Stoddart Publishing Co. Limited
34 Lesmill Road, Toronto, Canada M3B 2T6
180 Varick Street, 9th Floor, New York, New York 10014

04 03 02 01 00   1 2 3 4 5

Distributed in Canada by:
General Distribution Services Ltd.
325 Humber College Blvd.
Toronto, Ontario M9W 7C3
Tel. (416) 213-1919
Fax (416) 213-1917
Email cservice@genpub.com

Distributed in the United States by:
General Distribution Services Inc.
4500 Witmer Industrial Estates
Niagara Falls, New York 14305-1386
Toll-free Tel. 1-800-805-1083
Toll-free Fax 1-800-481-6207
Email gdsinc@genpub.com

Canadian Cataloguing in Publication Data

Gulliver, R. J. (Randall J.)
The Net user's guide to buying, selling, and trading collectibles

(Gulliver's collectibles)
ISBN 0-7737-6108-X

1. Collectors and collecting — Computer network resources.
2. Collectibles — Computer network resources.
I. Title. II. Series: Gulliver, R. J. (Randall J.). Gulliver's collectibles

AM231.G84 2000   025.06'790132   C99-933124-8

U.S. Cataloging in Publication Data (Library of Congress Standards)

Gulliver, R. J., 1951–
The net user's guide to buying, selling, and trading collectibles/
R. J. Gulliver. – 1st ed.
[184]p. : ill.; cm.   (Gulliver's Collectibles)   Includes Index.
Summary: Includes auction sites, message boards,
private collectors, and navigating and creating web sites.
ISBN 0-7737-6108-X (pbk.)
1. Internet marketing. 2. Electronic commerce.
3. Collectors and collecting – Computer network resources.
4. Selling – Collectibles. I. Title. II. Series.

658.8/ 00285 21 2000   CIP

Netscape Communicator browser window and menus
©1999 Netscape Communications Corporation. Used with permission.

Cover design: Bill Douglas @ The Bang
Text design and page composition: Joseph Gisini /Andrew Smith Graphics Inc.

THE CANADA COUNCIL | LE CONSEIL DES ARTS
FOR THE ARTS | DU CANADA
SINCE 1957 | DEPUIS 1957

*We acknowledge for their financial support of our publishing program
the Canada Council for the Arts, the Ontario Arts Council,
and the Government of Canada through the
Book Publishing Industry Development Program (BPIDP).*

Printed and bound in Canada

For GMC

Contents

Preface

THERE WAS A TIME when finding that one obscure piece you needed to complete your collection meant you'd have to thumb through magazines about collectibles, comb the dusty shelves of second-hand stores, haggle with vendors at flea markets, cruise Saturday-morning yard sales, hook up with other collectors at conventions, or hope your great aunt — God bless her — leaves it to you in her will.

The Internet has fundamentally changed the nature of collecting. Buying, selling, and trading collectibles has never been easier. The secondary market is now worldwide, so it's possible to find almost any piece in a matter of minutes. But while there are more sellers, there are also more buyers. And the worth of a collectible is no longer determined by experts or price lists — the price fluctuates daily. A piece is truly worth what someone is willing to pay for it on a particular day, at a particular moment. The thrill of the hunt has been replaced by the thrill of the auction.

The realm of collectibles has become a complex set of searches, timing, placement, and strategies. Where do you find rare pieces? How do you get the best deals? How do you avoid fraud on the Internet? Where do you sell your items? When is the best time to sell? Is it safe to trade with a complete stranger? This new arena requires a new set of rules, and that is what this book offers.

There are bargains to be had, money to be made, and your collection to complete, so let the *new* hunt begin!

Acknowledgments

There's a fine "collection" of folks I'd like to thank for letting me pick their brains: Cynthia, Mei, Steve, and Joseph at Art House; Rod and Pat at Enchanted Castle; Paul and Bruce at Merritt's; Joanne Keough at *Collectibles Canada*; Diana Hefti; Bob Reilly; Ross Amyot; and Darryl Kirk. For their patience and advice: Frances Bartlett, Nelson Doucet, Jim Gifford, Sue Johanson, and Tim Wynveen. And Bill Cuff, for his invention of Biff Capon and for egging me on.

R.J. GULLIVER
NOVEMBER 1999

Why Do People Collect?

ON SEPTEMBER 19, 1991, hikers high in the Tyrolean Alps, on the border between Austria and Italy, discovered the frozen remains of a man. Forensic experts soon realized that they had made the European archaeological find of the century. The body, mummified by the extreme cold, was 5,300 years old and virtually intact.

This Copper Age man, who came to be known as ?tzi (one of those absurd, unpronounceable anthropological words), spent the next seven years in an Austrian laboratory before being turned over to the Italian government. He is now on permanent display in a new $10 million Ice Man exhibit in Bolzano.

In addition to his heavy winter garments, ?tzi had with him a full quiver of arrows, some flints, a bit of moss for kindling, and, curiously, some seashells. Near the top of a mountain, and he had seashells! He had probably traded for them in the low-lands, and was returning home with his treasure. Perhaps ?tzi was planning to grind the shells down into a powder to create a magic elixir, or maybe he was bringing them as a precious gift for his true love. We will never know, but one thing is clear: he had scrambled through treacherous terrain for several days, carrying something that he believed to be rare and valuable, something that would, in some way, enhance his life. Those seashells "spoke" to ?tzi, touched his soul on some level. To understand that is to understand collecting.

(Or maybe he was just plain nuts. Bewildered friends have accused me of as much, on more than one occasion.)

Throughout history, both before and after ?tzi's fateful trek, kings have commissioned artists to create their own private collections, while commoners settled for gathering beautiful stones they found by the wayside. The impulse to collect seems instinctual, and probably goes back to our prehistoric "hunter/gatherer" days.

"Why do you collect?" friends ask. "Because it's fun!" I reply. But there's so much more to it than that. When I am forced to explain my pleasure in collecting, I can easily rank what satisfies me about the hobby — I love the fine-art quality of the pieces; I love the hunt; I love having rare pieces; and I love the investment potential. Most collectors that I know feel the same way.

Millions of people collect for a myriad of reasons. Most enjoy an object for its aesthetic value. Its intrinsic beauty touches them somehow and lifts their spirits. Many people collect for nostalgic reasons. Their preferred collectible is associated with their childhood or with a past journey, and it conjures up happy memories.

Some collectors are not collectors at all — they are "investors," accumulating items they expect will rise in value so that they might cash in later. Then there's the "prestige" collector, who specializes in rare pieces only, striving to possess something wonderful that no one else has. That sense of exclusivity, I think, is tied into self-esteem — it raises the collector above the pack. Children collect primarily for prestige. They want to be the first among their peers with the full set of Pokémon cards. And, admittedly, there's a tiny percentage of collectors who suffer from a compulsion, who can't stop themselves from collecting an entire line and for whom a new piece brings little pleasure because they are already preoccupied with obtaining the next one.

The "call" to collect generally comes at midlife, which suggests it is somehow related to our sense of mortality — maybe we feel compelled to gather up life's little pleasures as much as we can when we sense that time is running out. I started collecting Lilliput Lane cottages, which are miniature architectural sculptures, when I was forty-five years old. A collection does have an air of immortality about it. If we view it as an accomplishment, then we might feel that we have left behind something worthwhile for posterity to consider.

Collecting holds many other pleasures. It's truly a joy to touch a finely wrought piece and marvel at another human being's craftsmanship. You feel as if you are holding a little bit of their spirit in your hands. (It's hard to apply this to, say, a PEZ dispenser, but let's pretend.) Watching your collection grow is very fulfilling: each piece has its own story of where and how you got it, and may bring back memories of how you felt the first time you saw it. There's the potential of making new friends as you meet fellow collectors at collectibles shops, trade shows, conventions, and on the Internet. Many collectibles increase in value, and over the course of twenty years your investment will probably quadruple. Your kids will like that. And then there's the solution, for your family and friends, to the question of gift giving — they'll always know what you want!

Like all hobbies, collecting becomes a life-enhancing experience. Sure, you could live without it, but it does seem to fill an almost primal need for millions of people. One fascinating aspect of that primal need is the difference between what men — "the hunters" — and women — "the gatherers" — collect. Generally, men collect items that are more difficult to find, such as antique radios or Roseville pottery. They will drive hundreds of miles out of their way because they've heard that a small store in some godforsaken town in the middle of Montana *might* have some Heisey glassware in mint condition. Women, on the other hand, tend to collect more accessible items, such as Cherished Teddies or Royal Doulton, but they tend to "gather" more of them. It seems that men are driven more by the thrill of the hunt than by collecting for its own sake.

Judging by his seashells, I'd say that ?tzi had had a very good hunt.

PART I

◆

The
Collectibles
Realm

CHAPTER 1

Investment Collectibles

Hop into your time machine. We're going back to January 1995.

A company called Ty, Inc., which manufactures stuffed toys for children, is about to stop production on one of its poorest sellers — "Peanut," a royal blue elephant. You spend a few days scouring local toy outlets, buying every Peanut you can find, and end up with 100 of them at $6 each. Then, looking like a single-minded Santa, you stuff them all into your time machine and off you go to October 1997.

Upon your arrival, you start selling two Peanuts a week on a fledgling Internet auction site called eBay. Over the course of the next year, you make $7,000 to $10,000 per week as frantic collectors pay as much as $5,000 for each of your $6 treasures. By the end of 1998, you are worth about $400,000. Not a bad return on your original investment of $600!

Did anyone have the prescience to spot this trend back in 1995? I doubt it. (Although I have wondered whether folks from the future really do come back and do things like this. I have a call in to Mulder and Scully.) Could this type of frenzy happen again with some other innocuous item? You betcha.

Don't be too hard on yourself for missing the boat on Beanie Babies. It was a craze that was impossible to predict. In

1995, no one could possibly have imagined that people would mortgage their homes to buy a collection of stuffed toys. Of course, Beanie Babies weren't really collectibles, they were a pyramid scheme: you would buy one in August for $100, and resell it a month later for $300. That person would resell it in October for $500. And so on.

This certainly wasn't Ty Warner's intent. He just wanted to make inexpensive, good-quality, cuddly toys for kids. And he did. But when the rocket took off, the company added fuel to the flight by releasing limited editions and variations, as well as by retiring characters quickly, regardless of whether they were selling well. It was an ingenious marketing approach that has become a model for many other manufacturers of collectibles.

Admittedly, the circumstances that led to the craze were unique: the economy was the best it had been in years; many people were just discovering the Internet; eBay was just starting to take off; baby boomers were entering their "collecting years"; and Beanies were well made and thoroughly loveable. It's a formula that will never be repeated. Instead, there will be some other set of circumstances that we can't foresee, although we can make an educated guess based on where we are now.

The Future of Collecting

If the economy continues to flourish — and the experts predict that it will — boomers will begin to collect items that have some "prestige" attached to them. Having been humiliated by the juvenile frenzy associated with plush toys, they will shift towards collectibles that have a long and respected history of quality and style.

Upscale porcelain items such as Lladro, Disney Classics, and Armani are good bets. So is crystal, such as Swarovski and Waterford. High-end paperweights, like those made by Caithness

Glass from Scotland, should become more popular. Collectibles made of metals, particularly platinum and gold, will develop a following. A good example is Artesania Rinconada. This line of surreal ceramic animal figurines has been made in Uruguay for the past thirty years, and some items are decorated with paints made from real gold and platinum. Computer-painted replicas of fine-art masterpieces by artists like Magritte and da Vinci are on the way. These duplicates, which are actually paint-on-canvas, are exact copies right down to the last brush stroke. And when collectors do turn to plush, it will be the established lines, such as Steiff and Gund, that will benefit.

All of these collectibles are relatively expensive, and that will suit boomers just fine. Meanwhile, younger generations, with less disposable income, will continue to collect low-end resin and plastic items. As a result, medium-priced collectibles, such as Harmony Kingdom, Lilliput Lane, Gene dolls, and Salvino sports figurines, will be squeezed out of the marketplace.

Another possibility is that collectors will reject the notion of permanence and choose to invest instead in "perishable" items. Boomers are very conscious of status, and nothing says prestige like spending a considerable sum of cash on something that can be enjoyed only briefly — for example, one-of-a-kind, "designer" fireworks. Perhaps more likely, given the rising interest in gardening, they will invest in limited-edition plants, such as personalized tulips or rare day lilies that do indeed blossom only for one day.

Further down the road, when boomers become preoccupied with Depends and bingo night at the seniors' home, their children will collect something that seems unimaginable now: DNA. It will be possible to own an entire set of freeze-dried DNA samples from, let's say, all of the astronauts who walked on the moon. The DNA will be taken from hair samples, and cloned into limited editions. Preserved in Plexiglas, each tiny vial will come with an elaborate, full-colour presentation kit, including the celebrity's biography and a certificate of authenticity. Sounds ridiculous, right? So did the idea of people mortgaging their homes to buy stuffed beanbag toys. It's all possible, and probable. Collecting rare items as an investment is certainly not new — the wealthy have been doing it for centuries. All the Internet did was democratize the process. Now, anyone with a modest income can have a collection of die-cast cars, McDonald's toys or *Star Wars* trading cards. In the past, you'd have to wait decades to capitalize on an investment collectible. Thanks to the Internet, you need only wait a few months, a few weeks, or sometimes only a few days to make a profit.

But if you want to play this game, be warned: you must be as prepared to lose as you are to win. Those sorry folks who paid $5,000 for a royal blue "Peanut" Beanie Baby are no doubt wondering if their investment will outlast the appetite of dust mites for cotton fabric. They may have to wait twenty years for the fad to cycle around again — if it ever does — to recoup their investment.

The secret to success in investment collectibles is to spot a trend early, capitalize on it quickly, and get out as soon as you can. If you are really good, you may even start a trend!

CHAPTER 2

Trend Spotting

WHEN YOU ARE LOOKING for trends, there are two types to consider — the short-term frenzy trend, like Furbys or Cabbage Patch dolls, and the long-term investment trend.

Long-term trends are easier to spot. They encompass quality items that rise in value slowly but consistently, year after year. They're the blue-chip stocks of the collectibles realm. Figurines from Lladro, Disney Classics, Hummel, and Swarovski have never depreciated. Nor have fine-art paintings, although they're beyond the means of most of us. Still, first-edition prints by well-known artists have good potential. The "blue chips" are not limited to upscale items. Some pop icons have moved into the same category, because of their longevity. Early Barbie dolls rise in value each year. Other characters with a profitable track record include Batman, Superman, and souvenirs from the first release of *Star Wars*.

Spotting a trend starts at your local collectibles store. Whenever you visit your favourite haunt, ask the owner what is selling well. And don't forget to ask what *isn't* selling. It pays to linger, so just hang out and watch what other people are buying. This will give you a general sense of what's hot, and what's not.

Every so often, the opportunity comes up to flip a blue-chip piece as if it's a frenzy investment. While you're at the collectibles store, ask the dealer if there are any Special Events coming up when "one-day-only" pieces are available. Better still, ask if any have been held recently, from which he has remaining stock to get rid of. You can often get a bargain on special-event pieces if the owner has overstocked. And if you sell such a piece right after the event, when demand is highest, you can make a good return on your investment. Don't hold on to these items, expecting the price to rise. In most cases, it will only drop, and then start a gradual climb that will take years to match the initial buying surge.

(I made this mistake with a Cherished Teddies piece called "Humphrey." Humphrey was a Special Event piece available only through designated collectibles fairs for just two days in 1998. I bought two for $20 each. The day after the event ended, collectors were selling the piece on eBay for $50. I sold one but held onto the other, expecting the price to rise. It didn't, and within a month my small treasure was worth only $20 again.)

Frenzy trends are another matter. These can be tough to spot, and the best way to start is to enlist the help of a ten-year-old. He or she would have told you about their passion for Cabbage Patch dolls, Beanies, or Pokémon long before the market heated up. And if you're like I used to be, you probably would have said a polite "That's nice" and forgotten about it instantly. Not any more. Now I listen.

Most kids get a "bee in their bonnet," as Grandma would have said, and spend their allowances and pocket money on small items they just can't live without. They want every pack of Pokémon cards so they can show them off to their friends. They're driven by the prestige factor; it's hardly ever a question of aesthetics. No Disney porcelain for them! Still, since the Beanies craze, even children are beginning to regard their collections as a means to pay for college. Unfortunately, they're mistaken. A bona fide craze, such as Furbys or Cabbage Patch dolls, doesn't

*Original release of "talking" Pokémon figure,
with Japanese packaging, that you should have stocked up on.*

come around again, simply because there are too many of the pieces in circulation. A frenzy requires a short supply.

A toy called the Tech Deck has the potential to become a frenzy collectible. Created by a bored twelve-year-old, these are miniature skateboards, accurate down to the smallest detail. They even come with miniature tools for changing the tires. The line comes in several series, each bearing the licensed logo of a successful, full-size skateboard company. There are six Tech Deck boards in each series, so kids try to collect all six. They learn to "ride" the boards with their fingers, and create their own jumping tricks. In 1998, the first year of production, more than 4 million boards were sold, at a retail price of around $5. The first releases had smaller production runs, since it was a new product, and they quickly became hard to find. You fill in the rest.

Retired Tech Deck board. Go figure!

Another good place to spot a trend is your local Zellers or Wal-Mart. These stores are the "trenches," the front lines where low-end collectible crazes start. You can bet they weren't selling Beanie Babies at Tiffany's! Check the toy shelves. Which items are low in inventory or sold out? Ask the sales personnel which items they have trouble keeping in stock. Find out when the next shipment is arriving, do your homework on the item, and then — if it looks promising — scoop up as many as you can. If it's a relatively new product, like Pokémon was in 1999, you may have to wait a year to cash in your investment.

Study the auction sites for trends. In the category pages, most sites list how many items are up for auction in each category. Seek out the categories with the most action. Determine how hot the bidding is. Sometimes categories will be crowded because many collectors are dumping their collections. If that's the case, bidding will be very slow. But if the bidding is hot and heavy, you're witnessing a trend in full swing.

Check collectibles magazines. *Collecting Figures* is particularly good at spotting trends early. They do the homework so you don't have to. Similarly, the World Collectors Net Web site offers a "Trends" update that tracks various collectibles several times a year.

Look to the past. Since many collectibles have nostalgic associations for collectors, trends tend to be cyclical. Consider what was popular twenty years ago, and start to gather those items at yard sales and flea markets. Right now, items such as *Beetlejuice* action figures or My Little Pony plastic horses are rising in value. Mint-condition board games, such as the first edition of Trivial Pursuit, are on the upswing. Even early computer games, like Pong, have a patina of nostalgia that makes them attractive to collectors. (Future game fans will want unopened first-edition copies of the computer game Myst, so plan ahead.) Since the arrival of digital video discs (DVDs), the larger laser discs have become a rarity and have good investment potential. Keep an eye on current popular entertainment as well. Although the 1999 episode of *Star Wars* did not live up to its original hype, there are a few items from its commercial onslaught worth salvaging. For example, some of the action figures: everyone bought a Darth Maul, simply because he had such a cool look. You should be buying the figures that nobody else wanted. Those are the ones that will be scarce two years from now when collectors decide they want the entire collection!

Then there are the movies that have a chance to achieve cult status. *Trainspotting* and *The Blair Witch Project* are both well on their way, and you'd be wise to stock up on items associated with them. One that you may have missed (but I didn't) was *The Mummy*. Its blend of tongue-in-cheek performances and spectacular special effects could give it a shot at future fanfare, and I'm gathering up all the action figures I can find. (Because it tanked at the box office, the paraphernalia is going cheap.)

The world of pop music regularly churns out "flavour-of-the-month" stars to stock up on. My two choices this year would be Britney Spears and Ricky Martin. If I were seriously into this field, however, I would load up on any and all Spice Girl spin-offs from before Geri Halliwell (Ginger Spice) left the group.

And don't forget books. They won't rise to stratospheric levels, but you can often find remaindered copies of current books for very low clearance prices. Public libraries often sell off used books for as little as twenty-five cents each, and those can sometimes be resold, depending on their rarity, for fifty or sixty dollars. Zero in on those picture histories of some obscure collectible — such as "redhead" Hummel figurines — and books about animals. There is always a market of avid animal lovers willing to pay big bucks for that rare copy of "Misty the Killer Rabbit."

PART II

Buying

CHAPTER 3

Buying on Collectibles Sites

WELCOME TO THE WORLD of choice and chance!

Do you miss that Wonder Woman lunch box you used to carry to school every day? Do you want that second Christmas angel for your set of Seraphim Classics? Do you wish you could find that Coalport Toby jug to replace the one your kids accidentally broke? Wouldn't you love to have that magnificent Caithness paperweight — the one with the rose in it — that you saw in Scotland twenty years ago?

Thanks to the Internet, all those items and memories are just a click away. Tracking down treasures has never been easier, but the ease of access presents its own set of perils: Where do you go for the best deals? Is it safe to use credit cards? How do you know the seller won't rip you off? Can delicate items be shipped safely?

If you're new to the worldwide marketplace, it may seem to be a chaotic bazaar of dealers, traders, hucksters, and auctions. This section will guide you through the choices and chances that are out there. Yes, Virginia, you can shop in your underwear and feel safe!

If you've got a specific collectible in mind, one of the dozens of collectibles Web sites is the best jumping-off point. Most of these sites feature message boards, each dedicated to a specific line, where you can buy, sell, and trade with like-minded collectors. Web sites also often provide chat rooms, where you can discuss your favourite hobby in "real time" — that is, "live" — with other aficionados. Both services are generally free, although there is a catch: most collectibles Web sites require you to register by providing your e-mail address before you may use their services. By doing so you may be authorizing them to send you junk e-mail, or to distribute your e-mail address to other Net-based retailers.

You may consider setting up a secondary mailbox on one of the many sites, such as Lycos, that offer this service for free. Then, when you have to sign up for something, give this address, not your main one. You can log into the second address at your convenience and delete all those electronic flyers you have no interest in. It saves you the annoyance of getting home from work and having to sift through a mountain of messages.

WHAT ARE MESSAGE BOARDS AND CHAT ROOMS?

A message board is a public bulletin board where anyone on the Internet can post a message for all to see. We'll look at them in depth shortly.

A chat room is a forum in which you can have live online "conversations" through your Web browser. When you enter a chat room, a small window opens on your screen, and you can type in comments and questions to the other people who have signed onto the chat. Because of the time it takes to type a line of text, the content of the conversations is always a little out of sync. It takes some getting used to, but the ability to interact in real time makes it worth the effort. Soon you'll be able to actually speak to people in online chat rooms — a virtual, inexpensive conference call.

Top Collectibles Sites

THE WORLD COLLECTORS NET
www.worldcollectorsnet.com
The World Collectors Net, based in England, is arguably the best site of its kind on the Web.

(In the interests of full disclosure, I should state up front that I have written articles and created graphics for WCN — all for free. That's because I believe in the integrity of this site. In fact, in 1999, I bought a tiny share of the company. So, feel free to take into account my acknowledged bias in any references to WCN. It simply is the best collectibles site that I've found.)

Established in 1996 by Darryl Kirk — a Lilliput Lane collector — it has more than ninety message boards, covering everything from PEZ to Lladro. Each collectible has its own introductory page, with a brief history of the company and information on current membership pieces. Collectors can buy, sell, and trade pieces on the message boards for free. This site is run by collectors, not an anonymous conglomerate, and it has a real grassroots look and feel to it. It publishes monthly updates, as well as an excellent online magazine featuring exclusive articles. There's a chat room that has chats about different collectibles scheduled at specified times, although these are poorly attended. Unlike the other sites, you don't have to register to leave a message on WCN.

WHITE'S GUIDE
www.whitesguide.com
Launched in 1999, this site is coming on strong. *White's Guide to Collecting* is an established book and magazine franchise owned by Collecting Concepts of Richmond, Virginia, and the Web site is an offshoot of that company. It has the beautiful corporate slickness to it that you would expect from this successful

group, but there is so much information on the home page that navigating the site can be bewildering.

The site offers a preview of their excellent monthly magazine, *Collecting Figures*, plus a range of other features, such as full-time chat rooms dedicated to specific collectibles and Show Listings for upcoming Special Events. However, the bulk of the site is dedicated to commerce. There's a marketplace, where dealers have paid to have their businesses listed and linked, and there's a classified section, where collectors can sell their items for a set fee. The monthly magazine offers exclusive collectibles, such as die-cast cars, that are produced specifically for White's, and which can be purchased through their Web site.

COLLECTORSWEB
www.collectorsweb.com
Ron McCoy is a collectibles expert from Tulsa, Oklahoma, who has been publishing the *Antiques and Collecting* newsletter since 1996. He launched CollectorsWeb in 1997 and has recently sold the site to ChannelSpace.com.

McCoy's newsletter is the mainstay of the site, and there's a plethora of good articles that are well-indexed and easy to find. Navigation is smooth, especially with the site's first-rate search engine. There are more than forty message boards dedicated to specific collections. The strength of CollectorsWeb is its wealth of information. One hitch — you have to sign up and leave personal information in order to leave a message on the boards.

YAHOO!
www.yahoo.com
A venerable — or is that venal? — online institution, Yahoo! has some excellent message boards and chat rooms for collectors. From the main Yahoo! page, click on Clubs, then Hobbies & Crafts, then Collecting. There's plenty of traffic on these boards,

so it's ideal for buying, selling, and trading. However, being Yahoo!, it has no background information or articles on the collections represented. Again, you have to register, and these guys love to send e-mail. Look out!

COLLECTIBLE-INFO
www.collectible-info.com

This site appears to be run by a dealer called "Mr. Bill's Collectibles," but the site is not a retail store. Instead, Mr. Bill has turned his enthusiasm for die-cast cars into a great source of information for die-cast collectors. There are regular updates on new releases from Ertl, Matchbox, and others, and you can find past information in the archives. A general message board is available, and you don't have to register. Good site for die-hard die-cast fans.

ANOTHER UNIVERSE
www.AnotherUniverse.com

Although this site has products for sale and no message board that I could find, it does have some excellent background information on the collectibles represented. As you might gather from the title, Another Universe focuses on sci-fi, fantasy, the supernatural, and comics. Sponsored by *Mania Magazine*, articles on "Buffy," "Xena," *Star Trek*, Japanese *anime*, and just about any current cult TV show abound. No registration required. Good site for those who know their Borg from their N'Borg. (Don't ask.)

THIS IS COLLECTING
www.thisiscollecting.com

This new collectibles site, which was fired up on December 1, 1999, has a decidedly British slant. Two of the founders — Darryl Kirk, of the World Collectors Net, and Lorne Spicer, a well-respected collectibles expert and author — really know their stuff. They've created an information site with daily news updates, coverage of U.K. collectors' events, and online exclusives only available through thisiscollecting.com. All prices are in pounds sterling. For message boards, they've cleverly linked to WCN's existing communities. Like its affiliate, this site should become a valuable source of information for collectors.

Online Mall Sites

Then there are the pseudo-collectibles sites. The following sites, with one exception, are essentially shopping malls that list links to hundreds of Web sites belonging to retailers.

COLLECTORS ONLINE
www.collectorsonline.com
Collectors Online, owned by CollecTech, Inc., of Burlington, Vermont, is the exception. It's a hybrid between a true collectibles site and a retail directory. It has no message boards or chat rooms, but it does contain links to hundreds of articles about different collectibles. There's a directory of more than 800 Collectors Clubs, the site is easy to navigate through, and there's an excellent search engine. The main feature of the site is the mall, which has links to more than 200 dealers listed.

COLLECTORSNET
www.collectorsnet.com
Owned by Digital Designs, a North Carolina–based Web site developer, this site was previously called AMCnetwork and it focused primarily on militaria. Now it claims to have expanded to cover a variety of antiques and collectibles, although when I visited it seemed to have only two categories: militaria and comics. Navigation was quite confusing because the "navbar"

(that little site menu at the top or side of the page) was inconsistent throughout. There were no message boards, but there appeared to be a general bulletin board; I just couldn't find it. Collectorsnet's main purpose seems to be selling and hosting Web sites for dealers. I'm sure they're nice people.

CURIOSCAPE
www.curioscape.com
Launched in 1996, Curioscape is based in Seattle, Washington, and is basically a directory. It links to more than 3,500 sites related to antiques and collectibles, most of them dealers. Although Curioscape does not host its own message boards, it does link to others who do.

SWAPPERS AND COLLECTORS
www.swappersandcollectors.com
Swappers and Collectors is a new site for 1999 that — in spite of its title — doesn't seem to encourage true swapping. "Swipers (as in credit cards) and Collectors" would have been more appropriate, since the site is another mall. It does offer collectibles discussion forums for free, but it is essentially a collection of dealers. Yawn.

Buying on the Boards

Now that you've got a small taste of what's out there, let's get on with the hunt. Chances are you'll get a better deal on a collectibles message board than in a collectibles mall, so head for one of those sites.

Generally, navigating these sites is a cinch. Find your personal interest on the opening page — let's say, for example, Royal Doulton — and click on that topic. If there's a search function on the home page, use that. This will take you to —

possibly — an introductory page, and certainly a message board.

Message boards are public bulletin boards — anyone can post a message here. It's not unlike the bulletin board at the local grocery store.

Royal Doulton China & Figurines Message Board

Welcome to the Royal Doulton Message Board at the World Collectors Net. Please use this board to discuss everything about Royal Doulton. If you make an error or would like message removed, please let us know at boards@worldcollectorsnet.com.

[Post Message]

If you've never dealt with a message board before, don't worry: nothing could be simpler. At the top of the page, you'll see a menu or a button that says "Post a Message." When you click on it, you'll see a form that has blank spaces for your name, e-mail address, subject, and message. Fill it out (most people just use their first name), and then look for the button that says "Post Message." Click on it, and voilà! The entire planet can see what you've written. Beats the grocery store for coverage.

Post a Message!

Name: `Marco`
Email: `mpolo@venice.com`

Subject: `Looking for China`
Message:

`I am looking for a new trade route. Anyone know the way to China? Thanks!`

[Post Message] [Clear Form]

Messages normally stay posted for thirty days, so you can scroll through the past month's worth of messages. You will notice that the same few people have posted the bulk of the messages. These are collectors who frequently use this site. For them, the message board has essentially become a neighbourhood where they hang out. They communicate with other collectors on the board, sharing information, often buying, selling, and trading with each other. These are the people that you want to deal with. They will be the most reliable and honest traders, because the "neighbourhood" is small, and none of them can afford to have his or her reputation ruined by a bad business deal.

That's the beauty of a message board — for the most part, it's a self-policing community. Unreliable traders are soon exposed, and everyone else simply ignores their messages — in a sense, they become "invisible" to the other collectors. Occasionally, some nasty sniping will break out between community members. This is great fun to watch, but if it goes too far the Webmaster who oversees the site may step in and put a stop to it. Boneheads can be electronically "banished" from the board forever.

If the object of your desire is not listed, then post a message stating what you are looking for, and be sure to leave your e-mail address. In this particular case, though, you are in luck! You notice that one of the regulars is selling the figurine you've been lusting after. She's asking $150 plus shipping, which you feel is a reasonable price. Now what do you do?

First off, remember that prices on the Internet are generally quoted in U.S. dollars, unless otherwise specified. Converting that list price into your local currency may dampen your enthusiasm. For example, if you are in Canada, the "reasonable" price just went up 50 percent. As for shipping, where will the item be shipping from? If the seller is in Hong Kong, this could add another $50 to the price.

You will find her e-mail address with her message. Contact her, and determine some pertinent facts: Is the piece in mint condition? Where will she be shipping from and what will be the approximate cost? Will it be insured for damage and loss? Would she be willing to take less money for it? Can she give you two references from past dealings? Is she registered on an auction site where you can check her rating?

After checking her references and ratings (not foolproof, but generally helpful), you decide that she seems trustworthy. She has responded that the piece is in mint condition, shipping and insurance will be US$10, and she is willing to entertain a lower offer. You write back and offer US$125 for the figurine, and she accepts. The deal is struck, and you are the proud owner of that rare figurine you've always wanted. Now the most maddening part of the transaction takes place!

You send off your international money order and wait. And then wait some more. If she's a good trader, she will notify you by e-mail when your payment arrives, and let you know when she will ship your piece. Then you wait. After being spoiled by the immediacy of the Internet, this process seems interminable. If all goes smoothly, it will take two to four weeks to complete the transaction. Typically, by the time your precious package arrives, you will have forgotten what it was you ordered.

Corporate Message Boards

In a new trend, companies that sell collectibles — such as Coca-Cola, Royal Doulton, and Collectible World Studios, which makes "Pocket Dragons" — have started hosting their own message boards on their corporate sites. Not only is it an effective way to maintain brand loyalty, it's also a sign that these companies have realized the effect of the secondary market on the primary market. Here's how it works.

Let's say Coca-Cola releases an item, such as a stuffed animal holding a miniature Coca-Cola bottle, as a limited edition of 25,000 pieces. It retails for $10. There are thousands, if not millions, of Coca-Cola collectors all over the world, many of whom would want one of these toys. The 25,000 pieces virtually fly off store shelves, and the entire run is exhausted in a matter of days. Coke makes a very quick profit in a very short time. But it doesn't stop there.

Within hours, the cuddly critters start showing up for sale on message boards and auction sites, with secondary prices ranging from $20 to $50. While those collectors who purchased on the primary market make a tidy profit, the perception that Coke items are hot ripples throughout the secondary market. (That belief works to Coca-Cola's advantage.)

Collectors start buying up other Coke products, expecting them to rise in value, too. And they will, simply because people are buying them up. It's a self-fulfilling prophecy. Coca-Cola can now release its second batch of critters at a higher retail price of, say, $15 and be assured that it, too, will sell out.

This is brilliant marketing (they must have fired that guy who came up with the new Coke formula) and it makes sense for companies to promote the secondary market directly. It attracts collectors to the Web site and improves the value of their items on the primary market.

Connecting with Dealers

There are thousands of secondary-market dealers on the Internet, ranging from established stores to private collectors who sell pieces to finance their own collections. But how do you find them?

Often, the bigger dealers advertise by placing banners (those flashing ads across the top of the screen) on message boards. Many of the shopping mall–type sites host "virtual" storefronts for dealers. These sites have their own search engines, and will sort through the stores for you, looking for whatever collectible you've selected. Probably the easiest way to start your hunt, though, is with the search function on your own browser. It will pull up many different dealers for you, including private dealers who have gone to the trouble of listing their sites with the Web databases. You can also track down dealers through the pseudo-collectibles sites I've mentioned previously. Many of those sellers will happily put you on their e-mail flyer list.

Although you may find what you're looking for at a dealer's site, you won't necessarily find the best deal. You'll likely save some money by buying through a message board or in an auction. However, dealing with a large, established store gives you a couple of advantages: reliability and the option of paying by credit card.

CREDIT CARD TRANSACTIONS

The idea of giving out your credit card number online makes many buyers jumpy, and often needlessly so. Consider the facts.

◆ Fraudulent use of a credit card is generally limited to a $50 deductible.

◆ The credit card issuer takes responsibility for any amount over that, as long as the cardholder notifies the issuer of loss or misuse of the card as soon as possible. This varies from bank to bank, and you should check with your issuer.

Buyers have a fear that when they give out their personal credit card number the information will be snatched from the transmission lines before it gets to the intended destination. Theoretically, this *could* happen, and it would constitute fraud. But it is unlikely. The time and trouble involved in grabbing stray credit card numbers is just not worth the effort to computer hackers. Besides, when you give your credit card number over the phone to order concert tickets there is the same potential it will be shared with others, and chances are you don't think twice about that.

However, with some credit cards, if you order an item through the Internet, and the company you gave your number to sends you twenty items instead of the one that you ordered, you could be liable for the entire amount. Again, check with your bank.

Secure Web Sites

Because of these concerns, "secure" sites have been created which use "encryption" technology. (Encryption basically scrambles your information, making it harder to intercept. "Decryption" puts it back together again at the other end.)

Many sites offer order forms for credit card usage. If the site is not secure, the order form will usually say so, but not always. How else can you tell if you're on a secure site? Version 3 of the Netscape Navigator Web browser usually shows the icon of a broken key in the bottom left-hand corner of the browser window. When you switch to secure mode, an unbroken key appears in its place. Internet Explorer and Version 4 of Netscape feature a small icon of a lock on their windows; it's locked or unlocked to indicate whether you're on a secure site. Another way to tell if an order form is secure is to look at the URL address. If it begins with "https:", the site is secure.

Incidentally, don't be fooled by insecure order forms that display your credit card number as a series of asterisks. Even though that's what you see in your browser window, the actual number — not the asterisks — is being transmitted.

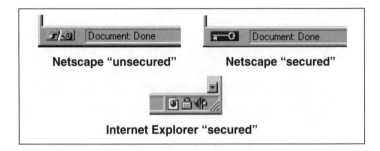

A simple way to protect yourself is to get a second credit card with a very low limit, such as $200, and use it exclusively for your Internet transactions. Keep a record of whom you give your number to, and when. If anything fraudulent starts to happen, you'll be right on top of it, with potential for only a minor loss.

In short, there is a risk involved in using your credit card to order an item on the Internet, but the risk is low — and even lower dealing through a secure site operated by a reputable dealer.

Private Collectors' Sites

There are thousands of small Web sites run by private collectors who resell pieces to support their own collections. Usually they will have no credit card facility. These sites have the highest potential for fraud.

Owners of these sites are independent. They're not part of an online community, so there is no one to police them. There is no mechanism for past buyers to leave comments. They may belong to a "good dealers association," such as the one sponsored by the World Collectors Net, that forces them to adhere to certain "fair trading" guidelines. If they do, they'll have a logo on their Web site indicating their affiliation. Even with that, ask for references and check them.

Odds are good that the small dealer also sells through an

auction site. Check into that, and review the feedback left by past buyers. People often use pseudonyms on auction sites, so check to see that the e-mail address matches the dealer's just in case he gave you someone else's name to review, someone with good feedback. Believe me, it happens.

Spending the time to do a thorough evaluation before you send off your hard-earned cash could save you a lot of heartache later. I have to point out, though, that in the hundreds of Internet dealings that I have had, I have never been ripped off once. It's been a pleasant surprise to discover that people are generally far more honest than they are given credit for.

CHAPTER 4

Buying at Auctions

IN THE PAST, collectors groups — such as the one for Lilliput Lane — would stage an annual auction for rare and retired pieces. The prices set at that auction would determine the value of individual pieces for the following year, until the next auction.

On the Internet, auctions go on twenty-four hours a day, every day of the year. Prices fluctuate daily, and investors trade collectibles like stocks.

The big kahuna of auction sites is eBay. Started by a PEZ collector trying to expand his wife's collection, eBay is one of the great success stories of the Internet. Although it offers everything from refrigerators to sex devices, eBay was built on the marketing success of a single collectible: Beanie Babies. Beanie collectors logged on by the hundreds of thousands when the fad was at its height, turning the site into the financial success it is today.

There are hundreds of other auction sites, many with their own merits — Auctions.com, Up4Sale (a subsidiary of eBay), Amazon, Yahoo!, Serious Collectors, and so on. We'll examine some of these in a later chapter. Auction rules vary from site to site, so you should always check the page of frequently asked questions (FAQs) before you submit a bid.

Getting In on the Auction Action!

To bid on an item at most auction sites, you must be a registered member. It's usually free to register, but some auctions charge a nominal fee, billed to your credit card. Once you've been granted the "privilege" of buying or selling, you arrive at the site's home page, where you will find a list of categories with items up for auction. Skip that, and instead look for the site's Search function, which should also be on the home page. Let's use a Royal Doulton figure, "Geraldine," as an example. Type in "Royal Doulton," and click on "Go."

Geraldine

The next page that comes up tells you there are 3,447 Royal Doulton pieces up for sale, and shows you the first 50. Unless you have plenty of time on your hands, you'll need to narrow your search. Type in the specific name of the figurine — "Royal Doulton Geraldine" — and let 'er rip. That's more like it — now you have a list of just five "Geraldines" to choose from.

CheesyAuctions.com
"If you don't sell it, we'll eat it."

royal doulton geraldine	Search

5 items found matching "royal doulton geraldine"

Item #	Item	Current Price	Bids	Ends
54092	Royal Doulton "Geraldine" - Ret'd 76 - Mint ✳ ✦	$47.00	4	12/05 13:10
54843	Doulton "Geraldine" - Only repaired twice	$03.00	0	12/07 22:30
55221	Geraldine - Royal Doulton - Lovely piece ✳	$24.99	1	12/10 09:43

In the left-hand column, you see the item's auction number, followed by a "headline" description of the piece. On the right you will see a dollar figure. That's the current bid — the highest bid at the moment — as well as the time and date the auction ends.

The first headline on your list reads, "Royal Doulton Geraldine — Ret'd 76 — Mint," and the current bid is $47. A little icon by the headline indicates that there's a picture to view, and another icon indicates that there is a reserve price (more about reserve prices shortly). The auction ends tomorrow. Click on the headline.

This will take you to a full description of the figurine, posted by the seller, and possibly a photo of the actual piece:

This lovely lady figurine - "Geraldine" HN2348 - was released by Royal Doulton in 1972 and retired in 1976. It is one of the few matte finished pieces that Doulton produced, and has all the appropriate Doulton marks and logos. Mint condition, with no cracks or chips. Happy bidding!

Sounds good, but there are many other bits of information on this page that you had better consider:

CheesyAuctions.com
"If you don't sell it, we'll eat it."

Royal Doulton "Geraldine" - Ret'd 76 - Mint Item # 54092			
Current Bid	$ 52.00 (reserve met)	Starting Bid	$ 25.00
Quantity	1	Number of Bids	4
Time remaining	1 day, 2 hours+	Location	Michigan
Started	11/28/99	Ends	12/05/99 13:10EST
Seller	wanda@lust.com (73)	High Bidder	bill@grouse.com (17)

What is the current bid? ◆ The search page reported that the current bid was $47, but on *this* page we see it listed at $52. What the heck is going on? Well, the program that updates the items page that you originally saw does not keep a "running tab" on bids. It only updates those figures every fifteen minutes or so. The current bid you see here on the item page is the true bid you have to beat.

How trustworthy is the seller? ◆ Most auction sites provide ratings for sellers. The seller earns points by successfully completing auction transactions and getting positive feedback from buyers. Beside the seller's name, you should see a number or an icon of some sort. If you click on that, it will take you to a page of comments left by former buyers.

It is ALWAYS a good idea to do this, unless you have bought from this person before. Someone may have a rating of 21 by his or her name, but when you check the buyers' comments you may discover that this seller has garnered 36 positive comments, and 15 negative. Ratings systems merely subtract the negatives from the positives. Knowing this, you may feel only half as good about dealing with this seller.

All sellers start off with a "zero" rating, however, and some-where along the line someone has to give them a chance. If the seller's rating is zero, you will just have to listen to your gut.

There are other safeguards. eBay offers insurance from Lloyd's of London against fraud or misrepresentation on items worth up to $200 — there's a $25 deductible. This service is free to anyone registered with eBay. eBay also suggests you use a third-party escrow system, called "i-Escrow"; the buyer pays the escrow company, which withholds the payment from the seller until the item is delivered and deemed satisfactory by the buyer. i-Escrow charges a fee of 6 percent of the selling price, which is generally split by the buyer and seller. Auctions.com offers its own escrow service, BidSafe; instead of paying a per-centage, you can opt to pay a small, flat rate every year.

How much time is left in the auction? ◆ While you were mulling over the previous two bits of information, time has con-tinued to march on, unless you're Dick Clark. Keep an eye on the time remaining; you'll find it at the top of the page. Click on your browser's Reload or Refresh button to get an update on the actual time until the end of the auction. (Most sites will also indi-cate that an auction is in its "final throes" on the index page you were on before, usually by means of colour or some odd icon.)

The time remaining affects how and when you bid, as we will discuss when we get to bidding.

Where is the seller? ◆ Remember the Hong Kong example? Sellers don't always say where they are from. They may put some-thing obscure like "The Big-Mouth Bass State"; other than warn-ing bass to stay away, this isn't very helpful. Unless it says otherwise on the page, you will be paying for shipping, so it's wise to e-mail the seller and clarify his or her location. Just click on the seller's name, and you should be able to fire off a question via e-mail.

Is there a reserve price? ◆ A reserve price indicates that the seller has set a secret price under which he or she does not have to sell the item. If the reserve is $50 and the highest bid is $49.99, the seller does not have to sell. However, if the reserve is met — and it will say so next to the current bid — the seller is legally obligated to sell to the highest bidder.

Reserves can be very confusing. On eBay, for example, if the reserve is $60, and the current bid is $55, the page will have a line that says something like "reserve not yet met." Not knowing what the reserve actually is, then, you bid $70. The current bid will jump to $60 and say "reserve met." That's because, if you bid over the "reserve" before anyone else does, the current bid stops at the reserve price. The other $10 of your bid will be automatically used to fend off future bidders. This is known as "proxy" bidding. If no one else bids, you get the item for just $60 — much to the seller's chagrin.

Bidding Strategies

Before you place your bid, there are several strategies to consider:

When to bid ◆ In our example of the Royal Doulton figurine, there is still one day left in the auction. A bidder looking for the best possible price will wait. A bidder who is more concerned about getting the piece than getting a good price will bid now.

How popular is the item? ◆ Check the top of the item page, and see how many other bids there are on this piece. In this case, there are four other bids already. In other words, the Royal Doulton figurine is not hotly contested — so far. There may be bidders waiting in the wings to bid near the end. This is known as "sniping." If you know your field, then you will have an idea whether or not this is a popular piece. For this example, "Geraldine" is not considered a rare Doulton piece, so odds are good that there will be only a few — if any — more bids.

What has it sold for recently? ◆ All auction sites archive prices from the previous thirty days. If you check these, you will get a pretty good idea of what a piece is going for in the current secondary market. Using the search function, type in "Royal Doulton Geraldine" and click on "Completed Auctions." You soon discover that in the previous month, "Geraldine" has come up for auction three times, and sold for $48 to $64.

What's it worth to you? ◆ Always determine what an item is worth to you *before* you place your bid. That's all that really counts in an auction, and only you can determine it. Ultimately, secondary-market price lists and expert appraisals mean nothing to the true collector. If it's a piece you just can't live without, you'll know what you can afford to spend on it.

Placing Your Bid

Finally, the big moment has arrived. No more procrastinating — it's time to move!

At the bottom of the item page, you will find a form for placing a bid. It asks for your name, your password, and the amount that you'd like to bid.

If you have plenty of cash, and can't live without the piece, then bid high. In our example, you desperately want Geraldine and have looked high and low for it. Money is no object, so you bid high — say, $100. If the site supports proxy bidding — and most auction sites do — new bids are added in fixed increments — fifty cents, a dollar, $5, and so on. In this case, the increment is $1, so the current price will jump to $53, and the remaining amount of your bid will be used to fend off other bidders until the auction ends tomorrow. If someone else bids more than $53, thanks to proxy bidding the current price will jump to a higher bid with your name on it. So if someone bids $60, the current price will jump to $61, and you will still be the high bidder. As long as no one bids over $100, you are safe to go do the laundry.

If money *is* an object and you are looking for the best deal you can find, then wait until tomorrow. Successful bidders usually wait until the last two minutes of an auction to place their bids — the closer to the end, the better. Why wait until near the end of the auction to bid? For the same reason you don't reveal your hand in a game of poker: you don't want anyone else knowing what you're up to. If you start bidding early in the auction, you are raising the current price every time you bid; as well, you're giving notice to other buyers that they have some competition. You place a bid, someone else outbids you, then you top him or her, and so on. In this scenario, by bidding consistently throughout the duration of the auction, you're really bidding against yourself. The best strategy is to let someone else be the high bidder until the end of the auction, then trump them in the last two minutes. The other bidder will be left with no time to counter your final bid. This will also keep the price lower and you'll get a better deal. With this strategy, timing is everything. Be aware of the current bid, but don't just try to beat that. All the other fence-sitters will be bidding at the same time. Instead, your bid amount should be what the piece is worth to you. Period.

In this case, it is twenty-four hours later, and you are down to the last two minutes of Geraldine's auction. The current bid is $58. There have been eight previous bids. You decide that, at this moment, Geraldine is worth $70 to you, and that's what you can afford. So bid $71. Most people bid in round numbers, and it will only cost you a dollar to top them. Otherwise, you'll miss out and end up kicking yourself.

You Won! Now What?

Congratulations! You've emerged victorious from your global quest to buy Geraldine! Now what?

All auction sites require that the buyer and the seller contact each other within three days of the auction's close. If either side fails to do so, the transaction may be cancelled.

Now, don't think you're going to get away with this if, on impulse, you bid $3,000 at the last second for a Barbie doll and end up regretting it. Ignoring e-mails from the seller will not make the problem go away! At the very least, the seller will leave you negative feedback — and the more negative feedback you get, the sooner you will be barred from the auction site. At the worst, the seller will sue you: as a member of the auction site, you made a legally binding commitment when you signed up to honour your bids. By not doing so, you will have breached your contract and are fair game for litigation from both the seller and the auction site. Bottom line: *don't* bid on impulse.

In the normal course of events, if you are watching the auction when it ends, you can e-mail the seller right away. Or, the seller may e-mail you. Either way, you will *both* be notified of the auction results by the auction site, usually within eight hours of the close of the auction.

After you have contacted each other, the onus is on you, the buyer, to get the transaction rolling. The seller will ask you to send a money order or personal cheque, usually within five days. That's impossible with international mail, and most sellers will be quite accommodating with their demands. Many sellers will not accept personal cheques, so you may have no choice but to buy a money order — in fact, this method is safer for you because a personal cheque gives the recipient two things you may prefer them not to have: your bank account number and your signature.

A good seller will also ask for your address in the first contact.

This serves a couple of purposes: it allows the seller to pack up your item before your money arrives, and, by revealing your address, you are reinforcing your intent to send your payment. If you welsh on the deal the seller knows where to find you so he or she can launch litigation. (As you've probably noticed by now, business transactions on the Internet are weighted against the buyer.)

Normally, the buyer pays for shipping. The seller should have a general idea of how much that will cost. You can choose between the postal system or a courier, although couriers are usually much more costly. Most sellers will quote you a fixed price for shipping, while others will actually package the article and take it to the post office to get an exact cost. Insurance is optional; you'll have to work this out with the seller.

You include the shipping cost in your payment, mail it off, and then wait. Contact the seller after about a week to see if your payment has arrived. If not, wait some more. Generally, post offices will not declare that mail is lost until three weeks have passed.

Finally, the seller notifies you that your payment has arrived, and that he or she has shipped your item. Then, guess what? You wait some more!

CHAPTER 5

You Have Mail!

APPROXIMATELY TWO TO FOUR weeks after you first won the auction, your much-anticipated package arrives. In your excitement, it's hard to resist ripping it open faster than a six-year-old can maul a new puppy. Take a deep breath, then proceed carefully.

If it's a breakable item, such as a figurine or plate, examine the box immediately for damage. If the box looks a bit banged up, take a photograph of it *before* you open it, making sure to show the damage as well as the fact that it is unopened. This way, if there's a problem with the contents, you've got proof that the item was probably damaged in transit.

Another thing to check for on international mail is a customs stamp. If a customs officer has opened the package, they will have either stamped or put a sticker on the box indicating that the contents have been examined.

Finally, you open the package. Your item has arrived intact, safe and sound. There is much rejoicing. After you are done ooh-ing and aah-ing, e-mail the seller to let him or her know the item has arrived. Then, leave the seller positive feedback on the auction site, and ask him or her to do the same for you.

Case in point: I received this parcel, which was mailed from a city a two-hour drive away, three weeks after it was mailed, and in this condition. Some of Canada Post's finest work, I think.

Damaged Goods

But what if you open the box to find your precious piece is damaged? This can be absolutely devastating after the long wait. Here's what to consider.

How bad is the damage? ◆ If you're not fussy, it may be something simple that a bit of glue will fix. This is the simplest solution, and after a couple of weeks you may not even remember the damage existed. However, if you *are* fussy, or if the damage is beyond simple repair, you'll have to take action.

How well was the item packed? ◆ If it was packed poorly, with little cushioning material, then the seller is at fault. If the item was packed extremely well and the box contains no rubble from the damage, the item was most likely damaged before it was even packed. The seller either did not notice the damage, or has sold you a flawed piece after fraudulently representing it as being in mint condition.

I once found myself in the position of being a fraudulent seller, albeit unintentionally. I sold a retired Harmony Kingdom ceramic rabbit, which I believed to be in mint condition, to a woman in California. Upon receiving it, she discovered that one of the ears was badly chipped. She e-mailed me immediately, accusing me of selling her a flawed sculpture. I offered to refund her money if she returned the piece, and asked her to check in the box for any rubble. In the meantime I rechecked her rating on the auction site, and she had impeccable references.

She responded that there was no rubble to be found, meaning the piece was damaged before it was packed, and she offered to have the piece repaired if I would pay for it. I agreed, then went back to check the photo I'd posted on the site when I first listed the piece. Sure enough, you could see in the photo that the ear was chipped! I had completely overlooked it when I examined the piece and did indeed sell her a damaged sculpture. After much apologizing and grovelling on my part, she kindly accepted that I had made a simple mistake, and I promised to get a pair of bifocals as soon as possible.

Was it opened by customs? ◆ Customs personnel are not known for their fine repacking abilities, and an item could have been damaged by them, or after they were done with it. Customs officers generally cannot be held responsible for any damage they cause when they examine an item. If the package has been opened by customs, you have very little recourse for damaged goods.

Is it insured? ◆ If you're using regular mail, the answer to this question varies from country to country. The U.S. Postal Service will insure for damage and/or loss at an additional cost. This applies to domestic and international mail. Canada Post automatically insures first-class mail for loss up to $100 both domestically and internationally, and additional insurance is available. However, international mail originating in Canada is only insured against loss — *not damage*. In Britain, the Royal Mail doesn't insure international mail at all against loss or damage. For a fee, it will insure International Recorded (registered) mail up to £28.50.

There are no international standards, and you would be wise to ask the seller right off the top what his postal insurance does and does not cover.

Courier companies will insure for loss and damage on all domestic deliveries. Some, but not all, couriers will also insure international deliveries against loss and damage at an exorbitant additional cost. However, if you are receiving a rare collectible, such as a set of Limoges china, it may be worth the added expense.

WHAT TO DO ABOUT DAMAGED GOODS

After you've assessed the damage, the first step is to notify the seller. A good seller will respond immediately, often with a plan for compensation.

If the piece was insured, the seller should pursue a settlement at his or her end. Good sellers will usually refund your money right away, since the settlement process can take weeks or even months. The insurance company will want a photo of the damaged piece and a description of the shape the parcel was in when it arrived. This is where your photo of the unopened, damaged package comes in handy. Some companies will even want the piece back, so bear that in mind.

If the piece was packed poorly, you should make that clear to the seller. He or she will most likely disagree, but may refund some or all of your payment rather than risk a negative feedback comment on the auction site.

The worst-case scenario is if you suspect the piece was damaged before you bought it. This is fraud. You can express your suspicions to the seller, who will most likely deny them. Recheck the seller's feedback at the auction site to see if other buyers have left any negative comments about similar incidents. If the seller refuses to refund your money, go for the throat. Leave negative feedback, expressing your suspicions, and threaten to pursue fraud charges. It's a serious crime to commit fraud through the mail in most countries, and you should be able to pursue your charges through the post office.

However, if the piece was well packed and unopened by customs, and the seller's integrity is beyond reproach, maybe it was simply damaged in transit. These things happen. The seller has no obligation to refund any of your payment. The parcel left his hands in perfect condition and he has no legal responsibilities after that. As a seller, when this situation has arisen I've refunded half the buyer's money — that way we share the loss equally. This seems like the most ethical thing to do.

Do Your Homework!

What if your item arrives in perfect shape, but it's not the article that was advertised in the auction?

For example, I bought a Harmony Kingdom piece called "Sunflower" for what seemed like an incredibly low price. I couldn't believe my good fortune! But when my purchase arrived, I opened it to discover that it wasn't the Collectors Club piece I thought it was; instead it was a current, open-edition sculpture called "Sunflower." The club piece, the one I wanted, was called "*The* Sunflower."

Similarly, a friend of mine purchased a Lladro piece, which

"Sunflower" and "The Sunflower"

the seller — who had outstanding credentials — "believed" to
be one of a limited edition of 2,500. My friend later discovered
that the production run was in fact 5,000 pieces, a fact that
greatly devalued her investment. She wrote to the seller, who
admitted he was mistaken about the size of the issue, and sent
his apologies.

Both scenarios are perfect illustrations of the concept of
caveat emptor — "Let the buyer beware." Don't assume the
seller knows a collectible inside out just because he or she has it
up for sale. They may know far less about a line than you do.
Before you bid, do your research.

Researching a collectible is not that time-consuming. The
World Collectors Net is a good place to start, since every col-
lectible listed has a page that features a short history of the item.
Plus, there are the message boards, which are viewed daily by

experts in that particular line. If you have a question, post it to the board and odds are good you will get two or three well-informed responses.

You can also use auction sites for research. Search current and completed auctions for the same item you are considering a bid on. Is the information about the piece consistent in all the listings? A search for "Sunflower" would have revealed both versions listed for auction, and eliminated the confusion.

If my friend had checked the Lladro piece described above, she would have found out that the piece was part of a limited edition of 5,000. She could also have simply gone to the company's Web site — www.lladro.org — and found the same information. Most companies have their own Web sites now, and you can often find them simply by typing in the company's name in your browser's Address window.

If you are researching the pedigree of a book, you can check with the Library of Congress — http://rs6.loc.gov/amhome.html — or the Advanced Book Exchange at www.abebooks.com. This site lists thousands of rare books for sale, and is an excellent source of information about first editions and original publishers.

Although my friend and I may have felt duped in these examples, there really was no recourse. The Sunflower I got was the one I bought, and the seller in the second case made it clear that he "believed" the size of the issue was 2,500. The sellers were under no obligation to refund the money — and they didn't. We will all bid more wisely in the future.

The Downside of Auctions

Using an auction site can be a positive experience. There's the thrill of the auction, the opportunity to find rare pieces, and the potential for bargains. But there are some negative factors to consider as well.

Most importantly, before you place that bid, think about what your purchase will do to local retailers. When you buy from the global marketplace, you stop shopping at your neighbourhood collectibles stores. Many of these stores have spent years developing relationships with collectors, providing an outlet for all sorts of lines. They're showrooms where you can see your collectibles up close, and touch and examine them in a way you will never be able to do on the Internet.

At some point in the near future, those local shops will be gone, and the only way you'll be able to see a piece before you buy it will be as a two-dimensional picture on your computer screen. Not quite the same thrill as holding it in your hands.

It's the classic "use it or lose it" scenario. And yet, it is hard to pass up a good deal on the Internet. The sensible thing to do is spread your purchases around. Your local shop may charge more for a certain item, but you can always compensate by getting a fabulous bargain over the Web.

Less obvious is the effect that auction sites have had on the secondary market. Over the last couple of years, auctions have, without exception, driven down the secondary market prices of all collectibles. Even Beanie Babies, the igniters of eBay, have fallen on hard times. Collectors who've spent decades building their investment in, let's say, Wedgwood have seen the value of their collections plummet. One could argue that the collections were overvalued to begin with, but that doesn't provide much solace to the "deflated" collector.

So, although collectibles and auction sites have made collecting easier than ever, they have also made it less attractive as an investment opportunity. It's a good idea to follow the "golden rule of collecting" that the clerk gave me when I was agonizing over my first Lilliput Lane purchase — "Buy it because you love it." Simple and true.

SECRETS OF THE BIDDING WARS — WHAT NO ONE ELSE WILL TELL YOU

Bid in the last thirty seconds ◆ As discussed, the closer to the end of the auction, the better the deals.

Bid when everyone else is asleep ◆ If you are on the east coast of North America, the best time to bid is early in the morning, usually around 6:00 a.m. eastern time. All sensible people west of the Mississippi are still asleep and folks in Europe are at work or drinking cheap French wine, so the competition is at its lightest. If you live in the west, your best time to bid would be 11:00 p.m. Pacific time. Easterners are asleep, and the Europeans are groggy from all that wine.

Bid during U.S. holidays ◆ Normally, bidding is very slow on American holidays (Memorial Day, Presidents Day, the Fourth of July), making them great times to pick up bargains.

Bid on off-nights ◆ Those are the nights when everyone else is watching TV. When *Seinfeld* was still on the air, this was Thursday. At the time of this writing it's Wednesday night. Keep an eye out for "big" television events, like the last episode of a popular show or the Super Bowl, and hit the boards then.

If several examples of the same item are listed, bid on the second-last one ◆ Other bidders will try for the first. If they miss it, they will wait for the last one. So, the first and last will sell for the most. Go down the middle, and you'll get a better deal.

Bid in the summer ◆ Prices always drop in the summer, mainly because most people have better things to do than sit in front of a computer all day. However, this is the season to make hay while the sun shines. In fact, this is a great time to pick up bargains you can resell in the winter, and take a few profits in the process.

Make a "Mercy Buy" ◆ If you see a piece that you like and it receives no bids, write to the seller after the auction and make an offer. More often than not, you will make a deal.

Mystical Auction Acronyms

MIB – mint in box
may or may not have been on display; comes in original box
with no flaws

NRFB – never removed from box
has never been on display, and sometimes has never even been
opened; often used to describe blister-packed articles and clear
plastic boxes, such as with Breyer horses or Hot Wheels cars

MOC – mint on card
another unopened, blister-packed article, such as PEZ

MOMC – mint on mint card
as above, but the card is in perfect shape with no bends or creases

NR/No Rsv – no reserve

Ret/Ret'd – retired
piece is no longer being produced

LE – limited edition
usually stated as a number of the total edition, i.e., #345/5000,
meaning Number 345 of 5,000

HTF – hard to find, i.e., slightly rare

CC – Collectors Club piece

PIC – picture

AE – Annual Edition
a piece limited to production of one year

DUTCH – duplicates of the same piece up for sale

FIN – someone from Finland

Cert/CA – Certificate of Authenticity

MO – Members Only piece
only available to members of the Collectors Club

Excl – Exclusive piece
only available in one area or store

PART III

Selling

CHAPTER 6

Selling on Collectibles Sites

W HEN YOU BUY PIECES, you can often get a deal if you purchase more than one of the same piece from the retailer at the same time. In fact, it's a good idea to buy several — especially true of rare or "Special Event" pieces — and resell the ones you don't want as a means of paying for the one you keep. You may also use an extra piece later to trade for one you want but don't have yet.

As you come to know more about the secondary market, you could move to another level — finding bargains at flea markets and yard sales that you can resell. Armed with your reference books and your secondary-market price lists, you go hunting for items that you know collectors will want, then reinvest your profits into your hobby.

Although Internet transactions are stacked against the buyer, there are also dangers in being the seller: the item you sold could be damaged in shipping; the buyer may leave you scurrilous feedback and ruin your reputation; you could lose money on a piece that you thought would be a sure bet; you will have to pay auction fees even though a buyer has backed out; you may make a substantial investment in a line that plummets in value before you sell it; and so on.

Still, it's hard to beat the thrill of watching that PEZ dispenser you bought at a yard sale for $1 sell for $200!

There are many factors to consider before you make your first sale: where to sell, how to sell, when to sell, and what to sell.

What you are selling will determine where and how you sell it. The first place to consider is a collectibles site, because it's free. As discussed earlier, collectibles sites have universal meeting places known as message boards.

A message board is the best place to sell a collectible. Although you won't get the exposure that you will get in an auction, the people who look at your notice are an absolutely interested audience. They only collect what you are selling. There is no better way to target a clientele.

The disadvantage with this venue is that potential buyers are very knowledgeable about the item you're selling. In fact, some viewers will know far more than you do about the line. Your pricing has to be exact, and so does the information in your posting. It is easy to look like a fool on a message board.

Pricing an Item

Let's say you inherit an Hummel figurine from your distant Aunt Gertrude. You're not particularly interested in the item, and it holds no sentimental value. You decide you might as well sell it.

Start your research. Take the piece to a Hummel dealer, and get some information. He or she will have catalogues where you can find out when the piece was first released, whether it is retired, and its name — which isn't printed on the base. The dealer may give you an approximate value, but don't count on it. Most dealers resent giving out appraisals, especially if you're not buying something from them. If you can't find a dealer with the information you need, you could try the Goebel-Hummel Web site. You may find the piece listed there. Your last resort is to post a message on a Hummel message board at Yahoo! or the

World Collectors Net. Keep it simple, so that your intent to sell the piece is not obvious. Most collectors are very honest, but some may lowball the value in hopes of getting a bargain out of you later.

Does Anyone Know...?
I have inherited a Hummel piece - stock #123456 -
and would like to determine some background information
about it. Name of the piece, release and retirement dates.
Any help would be appreciated. Thanks.

Hummel collectors who read your notice will either post a response on the message board, or e-mail you directly. If it is a rare Hummel, you will, most likely, also get offers to buy it. If so, you may decide to sell the piece right away. If not, you are now armed with enough information to do some pricing.

First, check the Hummel message boards for anyone offering the same piece for sale, and see what they're asking. If you can't find the piece listed, odds are good that it is either very rare, or very common, in which case most collectors already have one.

Your next source of information is an auction site. Check eBay and Auctions.com for completed auctions for this piece. These will give you an idea of what the low end of the price range should be. Remember that people use auctions to look for bargains — you won't get top dollar there.

Finally, to determine the high end of the price range, search for secondary-market dealers. There are hundreds of them, but two of the most complete sites belong to OHI Exchange (www. ohiexchange.com) and Collectibles Exchange (www.colexch.com). Both of these sites specialize in connecting buyers with sellers, and they have thousands of pieces listed in dozens of categories, with prices. Since the Web sites charge sellers a commission on any pieces that they sell, prices tend to be at the high end of the scale.

For this example, you found that your Hummel sold on the auction sites for between $160 and $200. On Collectibles Exchange, you found the same piece selling for $230 to $270. Average those out, and your piece should sell for between $180 and $250. Remember that Collectibles Exchange takes a commission on those top prices, so you should lower your high end to $220. You now have a realistic idea of what Aunt Gertrude's piece should fetch.

Go back to the Hummel message board, and offer it for sale at your high figure, but make it clear that you are flexible.

For Sale - Retired 1948 Hummel
I have piece #123456 - Boy with a Headache - which
was released in 1948 and retired in 1955 - for sale.
Mint condition. Asking $220. Open to offers. Thanks.

Someone may pay the amount that you are asking, but most likely you will get a lower offer. That's fine. Since you've done your research, you know that you could accept $180 — or even $160, since you won't be paying commission to an auction site — and Aunt Gertrude won't be rolling over in her grave.

Joining the Message Board Community

As discussed earlier, message boards have their own neighbourhood — collectors who use the board regularly for buying, selling, and discussing. Trying to sell a piece when you are an outsider can be tough. Make sure you have some references available for potential buyers.

Of course, you can use message boards to sell a variety of collectibles. It is often easier to make a sale if you sell several pieces as a lot. You are more likely to get an offer for five Cherished Teddies, rather than just one, because it looks as if you're selling off an entire collection. This is very attractive to buyers.

If you're a serious collector, and not some dilettante selling off a single piece, then you may as well join the community. You can make some great Internet friends on a message board, and learn about your favourite collectible from the experts. You'll share in rumours about upcoming pieces, find out about rare variations, and occasionally stumble onto a bargain. Plus you'll discover what the joy of collecting means in other people's lives. Besides, other than a hospital, where else do you have the opportunity to meet complete strangers while you are only wearing your housecoat?

CHAPTER 7

Selling in Auctions

THE THRILL OF SELLING a collectible at an Internet auction for far more than you paid for it is almost as much fun as finding a rare piece in a yard sale.

Again, there are many factors to consider in order to get the best price: your listing description, your graphics, the competition, the timing, the starting price, the reserve price, and so on. Just as in a real auction, buyers are looking for a great deal, so the highest bid that you get may be lower than the supposed "market value." But don't let that stop you. There's money to be made, if you know what you're doing.

To become a seller, you must register with the auction site. If the site charges a commission on anything that you sell, there will be a small registration fee. This money is applied to future commissions until it is used up. Although most registrants use a credit card for this transaction, you don't have to; you can register and send a cheque or money order to the auction company. After they receive your payment, they will activate your registration so that you can begin using the site. When that initial payment is exhausted by commissions, you will have to replenish your account, and send another cheque. Usually, you will be notified when your credit drops to the point of replenishment.

After you've registered, you're ready for some auction action.

Find a link labelled "Sell Your Item" or "Managing Your Auction" on the site's home page, and away you go!

Timing

In real estate, the three magic words are "Location, location, location!" In auctions, it's "Timing, timing, timing!" Knowing when to sell is the most important element of a successful auction.

First off, consider the seasons. Summer is a terrible time to sell on an auction site. People are gardening, vacationing, playing sports — anything but sitting in front of a computer. (On the other hand, it is, of course, a great time to buy!) Winter is the best season for selling. By January or February, many North Americans and Europeans begin to suffer from "cabin fever," and treasure hunting on the Internet is a wonderful escape. Plus, there are no garage sales or flea markets to compete with.

You wouldn't think that January would be prime time for selling; after all, hasn't Christmas shopping exhausted most people's credit cards? On the contrary, it is the highest volume month for auction sites. It seems as if collectors are treating themselves after being generous to others.

Just as you can narrow down the best months to sell in, you can also pick the best days: Mondays and Fridays bring the highest prices. In both cases, collectors are likely shopping as a form of consolation — on Monday because the weekend is over, and on Friday as a reward because the work week is done.

Even the time of day should figure into your calculations. If you end your auction between 10:00 and 11:00 p.m. eastern time, you will have the largest possible audience. For sellers, this is the "magic" hour. Folks on the East Coast are still up, and the West Coast gang has just finished supper and is looking for something to do. Why not help them out and let them bid on your auctions?

Finally, don't end your auction on a holiday, or a holiday weekend. The number of potential bidders is at its lowest on a holiday because most people have celebrations with family and friends to attend. Big television events, like the Academy Awards, can have the same effect, so keep those in mind, too.

Length of Auction

All auction sites give you control over how long you want your auction to run. This varies from three days to two weeks. Auctions.com even lets you decide what time you want your auction to start *and* end. This is a great feature if you only have time to list an item in the morning but you want to sell during the "magic" hour. On the other hand, eBay auctions run in twenty-four-hour increments from the time that you list.

The length and time limit you set depends on the item you're selling. Longer is not necessarily better: if you have a hot collectible, you will want to time your auction to end when there is the highest potential audience.

For example, let's say that at the height of the Beanie Babies craze you had a mint "Chilly," the rare polar bear with first-generation tags. Being a sensible seller, and realizing that the frenzy could end at any moment, you'd have wanted to reap your profits as quickly as possible. In that overheated market, buyers would not even look at a listing until shortly before the auction expired. The length of the auction would have no "bearing" (sorry!) on the final winning bid — only the timing was important. You would have wanted to sell Chilly on a Monday evening at 11:00 p.m. eastern, and you would have back-timed your auction to start exactly three days before — Friday evening at 11:00. Chilly, which originally sold for $6 retail, would have gone for US$1,500 to $2,000.

On the other hand, if you are selling a collectible with a

slightly better pedigree, such as a Swarovski crystal piece, you'll want as long an auction as possible. Upscale collectors tend to be older and, subsequently, more contemplative. They want time to mull over their bidding strategy. They also don't stay up as late. In this case, your auction should end at 10:00 p.m. eastern, or even on a Sunday afternoon when seniors are most likely to visit the auction sites.

The Competition

Before you place your item, investigate the competition. That will affect your timing, and your placement of the piece. Do a search of the auction site for the same item you are planning to list. If you find that several are already listed, you may be wise to hold yours back, or at least end your auction on a different day than the others. If you are determined to list your piece anyway, try to position it so that it is the first or last to go. You will get your highest bids in those positions. Another option is to look for a different auction site altogether. You may get fewer bidders on a less popular site, but you may also avoid competition.

Also, check the prices on the others up for sale. If they are all listed with no reserve, you're not going to draw any bids if you have one. Unless you feel you can get the money that you want with no reserve, you're better to wait until you have the sole listing on the site.

Categories

Auction sites always provide a range of categories for the different items, and most bidders will search only the category in which they are interested. (Savvy collectors will search the whole site, though, since pieces are occasionally listed in the wrong categories.)

When you are listing, you have no choice but to choose a category for your item. This is usually a straightforward decision, but occasionally you will have an item that doesn't fit clearly into any slot. If this is the case, find the category that matches it most closely. If the piece could fit into one of several categories, choose the one that has the most items listed in it; it will get the most viewers.

On the other hand, you can use categories to *avoid* competition. Let's say you have a Mats Jonasson crystal sculpture to sell. You could list it under "Collectibles — Contemporary," but you notice a similar piece is already listed there. You check "Glass — Art Glass" and find no Jonasson listings, so place your piece there. If it doesn't sell the first time around, you can change categories when you relist it.

Some auction sites will let you switch categories midway through an auction. So, if you're not getting any bids in "Glass — Art Glass," switch to "Collectibles — Contemporary" after three or four days.

Writing the Listing

Writing a great listing is an art in itself. I know a woman who could sell mosquitoes to campers. She writes the most irresistible descriptions you can imagine of her auction items.

There are two main elements to a listing — the "headline" and the "item description." The headline is the short title that comes up with all the other items listed in the category. It links to the item description, which is the full page the potential bidder goes to for more information on your piece. Both elements are important, but the headline or title is arguably the most crucial, since it draws in the bidders. It also contains the "keywords" that the search function looks for when a collector is on the hunt.

THE HEADLINE, OR TITLE

Auction sites allow a frustratingly small amount of space for the headline, usually about 35–45 characters, including spaces. You have to be very creative with what you cram in there.

Rule #1 is NO SCREAMING. Some sellers will write their entire headline in capital letters, which is the Internet equivalent of screaming. No one likes a screamer, and their effort to stand out usually gets them ignored, or even dumped from the site by the auction Webmaster. You can use capital letters, but do so judiciously. Usually a mix of lower and uppercase words draws more attention. Here's an example with a Lilliput Lane figurine:

LILLIPUT LANE RET'D "CATKIN COTTAGE"
(bonehead version)

Lilliput Lane "CATKIN COTTAGE" - Ret'd
(tasteful version)

Instead of using quotation marks, asterisks can make a piece stand out a bit more. However, unless you leave a space on either side of them, asterisks can confuse some search engines:

Lilliput Lane * CATKIN COTTAGE * - Ret'd

That's a serviceable listing, but you could make it more alluring with some additional information. In this case, you are selling a figurine that is in its original box and has never been displayed. So, you could add "Mint in Box" to the headline, and drop "Retired," since most avid LL collectors would know that anyway:

Lilliput Lane * CATKIN COTTAGE * - MIB

In addition, you are selling this piece with no reserve, a very appealing aspect to bidders. You could drop your asterisks, and add that:

Lilliput Lane CATKIN COTTAGE - MIB / NR

Now you have a headline that will spark the collecting passion of potential buyers.

But what if you have a collectible with a longer name? This is where being clever comes in. Let's use a Cherished Teddies piece as an example.

Even if the auction site has a separate category for Cherished Teddies, it's still a good idea to include the name of the line in your headline. Search engines do not look for categories; they look for individual words. Unless the buyer instructs the search engine to look only in the Cherished Teddies category, your item could be overlooked.

Let's say you've got a Cherished Teddies piece called "Hillary Hugabear" to sell. It's a retired Collectors Club piece, and it is in mint condition in its original box. You're offering it with no reserve. Lots of luck with that headline! Here's a solution:

Cherished T. HILLARY HUGABEAR CC/NR

I've dropped the word "Teddies," and replaced it with a *T.* The Search engine will still pick up the word "Cherished" and add the item to a bidder's list. To save space, I've omitted that the piece was retired, but will include that in the item description. For the same reason, I've also left out that it was MIB. Instead, I've listed the two most important aspects of the item — it's a collector's club ("CC") piece, which makes it more rare than an open edition, and there is no reserve.

For a popular item, you can use urgency as a selling point in the headline:

Beanie Babies MAPLE - 3 days only! NR

Exclusivity is also a strong selling point. Boyds Bearstones created a limited-edition piece called "Ewell & Walton" that was only available in Canada:

Boyds EWELL & WALTON - Cdn. Excl. LE

Humour can be a wonderful sales tool, and if you can fit it into the headline, you will draw some attention. Some people collect TV lamps, those kitschy lights that everyone had on their television cabinets in the '50s, and here is the headline I wrote to sell one shaped like a moose:

Vintage Moose TV Lamp - BIG & UGLY!

How could a bidder resist? Of course, they just *had* to see it. And bid on it.

THE ITEM DESCRIPTION

When a potential bidder clicks on your headline, this is the page they end up at.

Item descriptions are as different as the people who write them, but there are some general rules of thumb that you should follow:

Be concise ◆ Clearly describe the item that you are selling. Don't ramble and waste a viewer's time or patience.

Be honest ◆ If the piece has any flaws or drawbacks, make sure you list them here. On an auction site, you are only as good as your reputation, and honesty is the *only* policy.

Don't fudge the facts ♦ If you are unsure about a piece's origin or rarity, don't try to fake it. It's better to admit your limited knowledge on this piece rather than be taken to task by collectors who know the genre. Your credibility will be in doubt.

Accentuate the positive ♦ The entire point of your listing is to sell a product, whether it's a rare Minton vase or an autographed picture of the Backstreet Boys. Naturally, you want your item to sound as attractive as possible in your description. Emphasize the major selling points of the piece.

Be up-front about shipping ♦ If you expect the buyer to pay the shipping, mention it here. Some auction sites ask you to specify a shipping cost. Avoid doing so if you can. It's absurd to quote a shipping price when you have no idea where on Earth your item will be going.

Watch your spelling! ♦ You've got a spell checker — use it! Nothing makes a seller look more like an imbecile than bad spelling.

With those rules in mind, let's look at some examples:

If you are selling a common item — again, I'll use the "Maple" Beanie Baby as an example — don't waste the reader's time with a long, florid description. Every "Maple" looks more or less the same, with the only variance being the different generations of hang-tags. Here's the time-wasting version of the description:

Snowy white "Maple" is very cute and waiting for you! Ty Beanie Baby "Maple" is an exclusive Canadian bear, and is only available in Canada. He is extremely plump, with a beautiful red ribbon around his neck, and a tiny Canadian flag proudly displayed on his chest. This "Maple" has a 4th generation hang-tag with no creases or marks. I will include a tag protector with your purchase. He has been sealed in a plastic bag since he arrived. Definitely a museum-quality collector's item. Along with the other full-size International Beanies, such as "Erin," "Britannia," and "Glory," "Maple" is very hard to find. Add this rare Beanie to your collection today by placing your bid now. Buyer pays shipping.

This description is filled with basic information that all Beanie collectors already know. If, on the other hand, you're selling to someone from another planet, such a long-winded explanation may be necessary. A mere hint of hyperbole will do the job nicely:

Ty Beanie Baby "Maple" is the exclusive bear only available in Canada. Collectors' quality. Sealed in plastic bag since purchase. Mint 4th generation tag with tag protector. Buyer pays shipping.

The ever-popular Beanie Baby "Maple."

Consider your market. If you are selling a more upscale common piece, such as a Swarovski crystal "Unicorn," you can afford to make your description a bit more elegant:

A superb work of craftsmanship, the Swarovski "Unicorn" was the Limited Edition Collectors' Club piece for 1996. This beautiful crystal sculpture was released and retired in the same year. 4" tall. On the secondary market, "Unicorn" is valued at $600 - $700, and is an excellent investment. It is Mint in its original box, and has never been displayed. Buyer pays shipping.

Although every Swarovski "Unicorn" looks exactly the same, you have accentuated the rarity and value of the piece without insulting the reader with useless details. A collector of more expensive items is traditionally more contemplative. Generally, a listing for a Lladro figurine or a piece of Heisey glassware can be more literate than a listing for a PEZ dispenser or a G.I. Joe.

When you are listing a limited-edition piece, it's a good idea to list which number of the edition you are offering. Often, lower numbers in an edition sell for more money:

Harmony Kingdom "Have a Heart" - #316 / 2500 - is the original, banned Black Box. This Limited Edition was released and retired in 1998. Mint condition in its original box. Buyer pays shipping.

Rare Harmony Kingdom piece, "Have a Heart."

You may end up selling an item that you don't know much about. Rather than bluff, it's better to be straightforward about your ignorance:

Covered dish, "Hen on Nest" - electric blue carnival glass. 5" tall. I can't find a manufacturer's mark on this piece, and my knowledge of carnival glass is limited. Possibly, it was made by the Indiana Glass Company or Westmoreland. It is in Mint condition. Buyer pays shipping.

"Hen on nest"; unmarked carnival glass.

What if your piece is not in perfect shape? Minor damage on a piece doesn't necessarily mean it's worthless. If Shakespeare's original script for *Macbeth* turned up with coffee stains on it, would you turn it down? I don't think so. Many collectibles are children's toys that were played with and enjoyed, as they should have been. A few minor nicks and scuffs won't devalue a piece too much. Just make sure you describe the flaws as accurately as you can, or you'll pay for it later.

In the world of collecting, there are generally accepted terms that describe condition. These terms are far from precise, but they give the reader some basic parameters. *Mint* means that the piece looks exactly as it did when it was packaged at the factory. *Excellent* indicates near-perfect condition, although the piece may have lost some of its lustre from being displayed for a while. *Very good* indicates some minor flaw. *Good* means that the piece has had more serious damage, and may have been repaired, but looks fine to the casual observer.

Retired Breyer Traditional horse "Misty." In very good shape, with some minor wear on the front edge of each hoof. There is a small line approximately ½" long on the upper rear right flank that appears to be a pen mark. Otherwise, the piece is fine. No original box. Buyer pays shipping.

An item that has been repaired is a different story. It's not uncommon for a porcelain figurine to have a hand or head knocked off over the course of its lifetime, and most people fix it themselves with household glue. Inevitably, unless the repair was done professionally, a tiny crack will show. This sort of damage greatly devalues a piece, and bidders need to know about it before they place a bid.

Finally, it's a plus to inject some humour into your listing. Cruising auction sites can be a mind-numbing experience, and cheering up a viewer with a gag will make your listing stand out from the crowd. Here was the listing for the moose TV lamp:

From the bygone days of really big television consoles comes this vintage Moose TV lamp. Big and ugly! Over 18" tall and 15" long, it depicts a proud moose standing on a rocky crag. Ceramic, although the antlers are inexplicably made of plastic. Mixed media, I guess. I can't find a manufacturer's name anywhere on the piece, so I guess no one would own up to it. The word "Canada" is boldly displayed in gold lettering on the front base. A shotgun and an English hunting horn are lying at the moose's front feet. Presumably the hunter has been stomped to death off-screen. In excellent condition. Buyer pays shipping, which will be expensive due to the weight of this cheesy masterpiece.

ADDING PICTURES

I discovered in high school that a picture in the middle of my essay did not, in fact, add a thousand words. But in an auction, a picture can add to your profits. According to auction site statistics, items with photographs get the most, and the highest, bids. A listing with a picture typically gets 50 percent more bids than one without.

The most difficult thing to explain to a novice is how to add a picture to a listing. That's because you don't actually add the graphic to your listing — you add the URL, or Web address, of where your picture is. Then, when someone clicks on your headline, the item description page calls up the picture from wherever you have stored it. In other words, your photo is not on the auction site with your listing — it is somewhere else. Think of it as "call forwarding."

Photographs take up an enormous amount of memory

space. An auction site may have 2 million items listed on it at any given time. The amount of computer server space required to store that many pictures would be overwhelming. It can be done, but the auction site would need a much larger server — which would, of course, eat into its profits. By having sellers store their graphics hither and yon, it spreads the burden over hundreds of different computers, and costs the auction site nothing. Some auction sites will actually charge you extra to add a photo to your listing. And you thought the banks were bad!

Let's start with the basics: Take a picture of whatever it is you're selling. It's as simple as that. Make sure the background is uncluttered — a white wall with a matte finish works well — and feature your piece from its best angle. If you have a digital camera, you can upload, or transfer, your photo to your computer right away. The rest of us will have to get the film developed first.

For an added fee, photo finishers will transfer your pictures to a CD-ROM or floppy disk. Otherwise you'll need a scanner to make digital copies of your pictures. A serviceable, no-frills scanner can be had for around $100. If you have a scanner you may be able to use existing photos from catalogues instead of taking your own. However, you could run afoul of the copyright laws by doing this. Although I've never heard of this happening, the company that issued the catalogue owns the artwork that's in it, and theoretically could get nasty if you pilfered it for your listing. It's safer to use your own photos.

You will want to save your photos as JPEG (pronounced JAY-peg) or .jpg files. Save graphics such as logos in the GIF (pronounced JIFF) file format. Your scanner's supporting software gives you these options.

The software that came with your scanner, or a graphics program such as Photoshop or Paint Shop Pro, will also allow you to crop the photo to an appropriate size. Many programs will also let you alter the resolution — images to be displayed on the Internet should have a resolution of 72 dots per inch. It's important that you make the file as small as you can. JPEGs can take a long time to download, and you can bet that your bidder will be long gone if he has to wait for a four-by-six-inch picture to materialize. Make the photo as small as it can be, while still large enough to do its job.

Now comes the hard part — finding a place on the Internet to store the photo.

Most Internet service providers (ISPs) allow you a small amount of space on their server where you can set up your own home page or Web site. This is included in your monthly service fee. It's a good spot to store your photo. Essentially, you will be "parking" your image on their server, where it will be available to all viewers — including the auction site — twenty-four hours a day.

If you have a stingy ISP that doesn't provide space on its server, you'll have to find somewhere else to park your photo. Luckily, there are some sites that will give you a small space on their servers for free. Angelfire (www.angelfire.com) and Geocities (www.geocities.com) are the two largest. They make their money by selling advertising banners on their Web sites. Since they are giving you the space for free, be kind and visit their sponsors once in awhile.

Once you determine where you will store your image, you have to get it there. If you are using your own ISP's server, you should look at their Web site for instructions on how to upload the image. Both Angelfire and Geocities provide clear instructions on this process, but here's a brief rundown.

Initially, you set up your own "directory," or folder. On Angelfire, the URL, or Web address, for your directory would look something like this:

http://www.angelfire.com/hobbies/johndoe/index.html

You've placed yourself in the "hobbies" section of Angelfire, your name is John Doe (sure it is), "index" is usually used to denote the first page of a Web site, and "html" is the language in which Internet pages are written. More about HTML later, when you are better rested.

You now have a directory, or Web page, to which you can upload your photo. Again, the server should give you some guidance in this process. On Angelfire, when you sign on to your directory with your password, you will find a button that says "Browse." Clicking on it will open a small window that displays the files on your own computer. Find the image that you want to store on Angelfire, select it, and then hit the "Upload" button on their server. Magically, your computer communicates with their server, and the image is copied to your directory on Angelfire. In fact, it will be stored in a special "images" file assigned to your directory.

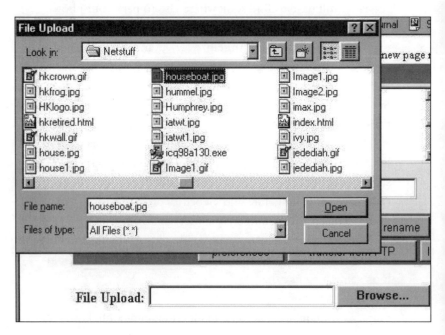

Let's say the photo that you're uploading is called "houseboat.jpg." After you've transmitted it, you can view it on the Internet from any computer in the world by going to

http://www.angelfire.com/hobbies/johndoe/images/
   houseboat.jpg

Take a moment to understand that address. You've gone to the Angelfire Web site, and are looking in their "hobbies" section, in a folder called "johndoe," in a file of "images," for a photo called "houseboat." Understanding the "path" of an URL will help you out later.

Now that everything is "clear as mud," as my grandmother used to say, all I can suggest is that you try it. Just remember that even people who collect *beer caps* have managed to figure this out.

Meanwhile, back at the auction site, you now have the option of adding a photo to your listing. While you're creating your listing, you'll see a blank slot for "Image." Usually the auction site will already have filled in the prefix "http." To it, you will add:

www.angelfire.com/hobbies/johndoe/images/houseboat.jpg

When you preview your listing, the photo should appear, and you can congratulate yourself on conquering the mystique of putting pictures on the Web. If it doesn't appear, check the address you submitted — a typo in the URL is the most common reason why this wouldn't work. Barring an error there, rethink the whole process, go have a beer, and throw away the cap just to spite them.

FOLDERS AND FILES

Maybe I'm a bit dense, but I've always found the computer lingo about "folders" and "files" to be a bit confusing. A *folder* is the same thing as a directory. It's like the drawer of a filing cabinet. Inside the folder, there can be other folders. A *file* is one item in a folder. Most commonly it will be a document or a photo.

THIS SECTION IS NOT ABOUT SEX

Now that you're awake, let's talk HTML. It's a great way to spice up the appearance of your listing without expending a lot of effort.

HTML, or "hypertext markup language," is the evil language that Web pages are written in. It was developed by those vengeful nerds you mocked in high school, but who are all now filthy rich. Don't panic; they actually made it fairly simple. At least it's in English.

When your Web browser, such as Netscape Navigator or Internet Explorer, loads a Web page, it translates the HTML code into the mix of word, pictures, and animation that appears on your screen. If you want to see what the HTML code actually looks like, try clicking on the "Page source" command, which you'll find under your browser's "View" pull-down menu. It's like a *Star Trek* episode where they get to see what the alien masquerading as the ambassador from Rigel IV *really* looks like. The horror...

In the chaos, some easy HTML commands can make your item description "sing." (Note: you are sprucing up the item description page, not the headline, which the auction sites won't let you alter.) Some examples follow. The bold type and other type effects are for effect, and aren't to be added to your coding.

To begin with, there's the very handy "bold." Just add <B> or <EM> in front of whatever it is you want to emphasize, and it does the trick.

<B>**Barbie - Version 1**</B> for sale.

With HTML commands, you'll have to tell the computer where the bold text ends. You do this by repeating the instruction, with a forward slash inserted. In this case </B> indicates the end of the bold text.

Want to add some colour? The basic colours all work with this simple command: <FONT COLOR=BLUE> — or red, or yellow, or green. Again, you have to "close" the colour by putting a forward slash before the word "font":

<FONT COLOR=RED>Barbie - Version 1</FONT> for sale.

If you'd like to underline part of your listing, simply use the command <U>:

<U>Barbie - Version 1</U> for sale.

The <I> command sets part of your message in *italics.*

<I>*Barbie - Version 1*</I> for sale.

Another way to emphasize a portion of the listing is to change the size of the font. The command for that is <FONT SIZE=+2>; +1 is standard; +3 is very large.

<FONT SIZE=+2>Barbie - Version 1</FONT> for sale.

If you want to get fancy, you can even change the typeface,

or *font*, used in your listing. The command is <FONT
FACE="helvetica, arial"> or whatever font you would like.
When the buyer's browser gets this command, it actually
searches the buyer's computer for the fonts you have requested.
In this case, you asked for Helvetica first. If that's not installed
on the buyer's computer, you've asked for Arial. If neither is
available, the browser simply displays whatever font it normally
does.

<FONT FACE="script, garamond">Barbie - Version 1
   </FONT> for sale.

Now you can really go wacky, and combine several commands at the same time:

<FONT COLOR=RED><FONT FACE="script"><B><U>
   Barbie - Version 1 </U></B></FONT></FONT> for sale.

One point — when you "close" your HTML commands,
close them in the reverse order that you laid them down. Some
browsers will crash if commands are out of order.

Using some basic HTML will greatly enhance the appearance of your item description, and is guaranteed to enhance
your sales. A word of caution, though: don't get carried away
with your new skills. Overdone enhancements, such as the
widely reviled <FLASH> command, can put buyers off. Use
HTML to make your description more attractive, not to show
off your programming finesse.

Adding HTML Spice to Your Description

`<B> </B>`	*Bold*
`<EM> </EM>`	*Bold*
`<U> </U>`	*Underline*
`<I> </I>`	*Italics*

`<FONT SIZE=+1 or +2 or +3> </FONT>`
Makes the font big, bigger, biggest

`<FONT COLOR=RED> </FONT>`
Changes colour. Works with other basic colours: blue, green, yellow, white, etc.

`<FONT FACE="xxx" </FONT>`
Changes the typeface that the copy appears in on the viewer's screen to whichever font you specify within the quotation marks

Remember: always close the commands in the reverse order that you have laid them down.

TO RESERVE, OR NOT TO RESERVE

Sellers often find the concept of a reserve confusing. In a reserve auction, the seller chooses a price that has to be met before he or she will sell the item. Generally, this figure is secret, known only to the seller. If none of the bidders match or exceed that price, the seller does not have to sell the item. Essentially, it's a safety net for the seller.

There are advantages and disadvantages to reserves. They can prevent the seller from losing money on a piece, but they may also stop bidders from placing bids. Being able to include "NR" (for "No Reserve") in your item description and headline makes it much more attractive to buyers.

If you are auctioning something that buyers covet and that you initially bought for a good price, there is no need for a reserve. For example, a Starting Lineup sports figurine of Babe Ruth may have cost you $10 in 1991, but now sells for $50 to $70. You could put a reserve of $50 on it, and undoubtedly get that price. But with no reserve, you will get more bids, which could push the final price up to $70 or more. Only you can judge the balance between your caution and your greed.

If you misjudge the market or mess up your timing, having no reserve can be a catastrophe. I once lost $200 on a retired Lilliput Lane piece because I misjudged the strength of the market. Live and learn.

What if the reserve is not met? No problem. You can relist the item, and the auction site will usually let you do it for free. You may consider lowering your reserve on the relisting, but this is not essential — maybe you'll be lucky the second time around. You don't have to relist immediately: most auction sites give you up to thirty days to relist, and you may want to wait for better timing.

To relist an item, you'll have to find your original listing in the site's "completed auctions" section. It's a good idea to keep a record of your item number, so that the listing will be easy to find. Go to the search area of the auction site, and simply type in the item number. That will recall your item description page, and you'll find a "Relist" option there. It's a lot easier than redoing the entire listing from scratch.

CHAPTER 8

Costs of Doing Business Online

Auction Site Fees

There are dozens of Internet auction sites and they are not created equal. One significant way in which they vary is their fee structures. As with anything, it's a good idea to shop around. Let's compare the cost of selling a $100 item on a few of the biggest sites:

EBAY
www.ebay.com

The all-purpose giant of the Internet auction world was started in September 1995 by Pierre Omidyar after his wife, an avid PEZ collector, expressed an interest in finding trading partners on the Web. It is now a publicly traded company, listed on the Nasdaq exchange.

eBay offers real-time auctions, whereby each item up for sale has a predetermined end to the bidding. As discussed under Bidding, the site allows proxy bidding, which means that the bidder names the highest price he will pay and the program automatically bids for him, raising the bid as needed but not exceeding the preset limit. Consequently, under proxy bidding, the seller may receive less than the buyer was actually willing to pay. Great for the buyer; not so great for the seller.

Your initial cost on eBay is a non-refundable insertion fee. This fee varies with the amount you set as your opening value, or your reserve, if there is one:

Opening value	Insertion fee
$00.01–9.99	$0.25
$10.00–24.99	$0.50
$25.00–49.99	$1.00
$50.00 and up	$2.00
Automobiles	$25.00 fixed
Real estate	$50.00 fixed

Let's say you're pretty sure your item will sell for $100, so you can set your opening value relatively low — $24.99. That will cost you 50 cents whether it sells or not. You could set the opening value lower — say, $5.00 — and save a quarter, but no one is going to take you seriously if you start too low.

Recently, eBay has introduced a $1 fee if you set a reserve price at all. In this example of a $100 item, you may be wise to protect your investment with a reserve anyway. So set the reserve at $100, bite the bullet, and pay the fee. You've now spent $1.50, and you're not even out of the gate yet. (After many customer complaints, eBay has recently changed their policy and will refund the $1.00 if the item sells.)

eBay pioneered a totally confusing commission structure, which has been imitated elsewhere. If you read it over, you may well get glassy-eyed and finally just mutter, "Whatever." Here it is in all its glory:

◆ On the first $25 of the final selling price, you pay 5 percent.
◆ On any portion of the selling price between $25.01 and $1,000, you pay 2.5 percent.
◆ On any part of the selling price over $1,000, you pay 1.25 percent.

If the reserve price is not met, or there are no bids, then there is no commission. But your piece sells for $100, as predicted; therefore, eBay takes 5 percent of the first $25 — that's $1.25 — and 2.5 percent of the other $75, or $1.88. So the total commission is $3.13.

In total, your transaction on eBay cost $4.63 — and when eBay refunds the $1 for your reserve, that's $3.63. That's less than 4 percent, and quite fair when you think about it.

AUCTIONS.COM
www.auctions.com

This auction site should be the giant of the Web. Formerly known as Auction Universe, it was started by Classified Ventures, which is based in Chicago and funded by eight leading media companies, including the publishers of *USA Today* and the *New York Times.* In spite of such heavyweight backers, auctions.com has had a tough time prying customers out of eBay's stranglehold. There now appear to be new owners or partners involved. Presumably this has resulted in the easier-to-remember new name.

Auctions.com has real-time auctions with predetermined closing times and proxy bidding. Previously, Auction Universe boasted an innovation that sellers certainly liked — an auction didn't end as long as people were still bidding. After the closing time, there was a grace period of five minutes for latecomers. As far as I can determine, the revamped site is no longer offering extended auctions. Auctions.com has another nice feature for sellers who really don't want to fool around. It's called FirstBidWins, and it isn't really an auction at all. You simply name your selling price, and the first person who bids wins.

Unlike eBay, the price structures on auctions.com are refreshingly straightforward. It's free to list any item at any price, and there is no charge for a reserve. The commission on all sales is 2.5 percent of the final sale price — so your $100 sale will cost you $2.50. Unfortunately, at this time, auctions.com does not have the volume of buyers that eBay does.

AMAZON.COM AUCTIONS
www.amazon.com/auctions

Sure they can sell books, but can they run an auction site? The online bookselling giant has copied many features of eBay and auctions.com — real-time auctions, proxy bidding, and time extensions if bidding is still active. On Amazon, if someone bids in the last ten minutes of an auction, the auction is automatically extended another ten minutes, ad infinitum.

Amazon.com, Inc., is a publicly traded company on the Nasdaq exchange. In June 1999 it announced plans to launch a joint site with the famed Sotheby's auction house to be called sothebys.amazon.com. With its huge database of customers, Amazon.com auctions will provide the real threat to eBay.

When Amazon.com started its auction site, its listing fee, on any item, was only 10 cents. That didn't last long, and they now follow the same listing fee structure as eBay. However, they don't charge extra if you set a reserve price. So your listing fee — based again on a $24.99 opening value — will be 50 cents.

Amazon.com gets no points for inventive thinking. Their commission structure also follows eBay exactly, so your $100 sale will cost you $3.63.

UP4SALE
www.up4sale.com

Up4Sale is owned by eBay, Inc., and is inexplicably free! (Must have been brought on by pangs of conscience over all the fees at eBay.) Sure, you can pay for little extras like "bold listings" and icons, just like on the other sites, but you don't have to. (A "bold listing" simply means that your headline will appear in boldface, making it stand out from the others on the list of titles. All of the auction sites offer ways to enhance your head-line — for a fee — including "Featured Auctions," which place your headline on a special list of so-called important auctions, perhaps even displayed on the auction site's main home page.

It's a great location for inexpensive items on which you really don't want to pay a commission. Up4Sale auctions are domi-nated by two kinds of items — Beanie Babies and trading cards. Based on this, I suspect that most of the buyers are kids, and they probably won't be battling over your Swarovski crystal.

Your $100 sale will cost you nothing, but remember, you get what you pay for.

YAHOO! AUCTIONS
auctions.yahoo.com
Yahoo! is publicly traded on the Nasdaq, and is primarily known as a *portal* site — an online "information booth" from which you can do an Internet search.

Like Up4Sale, Yahoo! charges no listing fees or commis-sions. Unlike Up4Sale, it has no enhancements of any kind — no "bold listings," no "featured auctions." The only auctions that are featured are those chosen by the Yahoo! staff, who seem to have too much time on their hands.

Although these are real-time auctions with predetermined closing times and proxy bidding, Yahoo! has an interesting vari-ation: sellers can opt to allow bidding to continue, or have a firm closing time. An odd feature is that sellers have the option of setting a "buy price." It's like a reserve price, but when a bid-der hits it, the auction is over. I'm not sure how this helps the seller since it ends the possibility of the price rising further.

Your $100 sale will again cost you zip. Like Up4Sale, the absence of fees tends to draw low-end merchandise, the kind of stuff you'd find at a garage sale.

THE SERIOUS COLLECTOR
www.seriouscollector.com

Launched in April 1999, The Serious Collector, Inc., is based in San Francisco and aims at sophisticated collectors and dealers who are interested in fine arts, antiques, and enduring collectibles. In other words, no garage-sale junk here.

A hybrid between a mall site and an auction site, The Serious Collector offers small Web sites to members who are professional dealers. Their auctions are unique in that they don't end for at least twenty-four hours after the last bid is cast, so "sniping" is impossible. Sellers can set an optional reserve price, and they must specify their own minimum bid increments. Items up for sale tend to be quite pricey, as you would expect from the founder's intent.

Frankly, I think having a site specifically for high-end collectibles is a great idea, and I loved this site. It's easy to manoeuvre through the clean, simple layout. It's the opposite of flashy. Even though the items up for bid are expensive, the listing fees are not:

Opening value	Listing fee
Under $25	$0.50
$25–100	$1.00
$100 and up	$2.00

The commission on the final sale price is 2.5 percent. So if you list your item at $24.99 and it sells for $100, you pay $3. Bear in mind that, given the classy surroundings, you should probably splurge and start your item at a more realistic price — in this case, let's say $75. Sure it adds another 50 cents to your cost, but at least you're maintaining your credibility.

CHAPTER 9

Going Once, Going Twice, Sold!

YOU'VE STAGED A SUCCESSFUL auction, and someone has won it with the highest bid. You both have three days to contact each other, or the sale can be declared void. If that happens, you will still have to pay the auction site its commission based on the bid, so don't think that ignoring the buyer's e-mails will get you off the hook. The auction site will e-mail both of you with the results within a few hours of the auction closing.

You don't need to wait for notification. As soon as possible after the auction ends, send the buyer an e-mail. Cordiality is in order, and your message should go something like this:

Hi,
Congratulations! You were the high bidder on the Star Wars figurine of Boba Fett for $32. Please contact me to make arrangements, and thanks for bidding.
Regards,
Sally Forth

Arrangements will include the cost of shipping, the method of payment, optional insurance, where the buyer should send the payment, and the buyer's address.

Knowing the buyer's address is your primary concern. That

will give an idea of shipping costs. A small article like an action figure can be mailed anywhere in North America for $3–$6. Courier delivery is obviously more expensive. If the buyer wants optional insurance, you'll have to account for that, too. As time goes on, you'll be able to "ballpark" the shipping cost of a simple item based on previous experience.

International orders, such as to Australia or Europe, cost much more to ship. The best thing to do is pack the item as soon as the auction ends and, once you have the buyer's address, take it to the post office or courier company to get an exact price. That way you will not overcharge or undercharge the buyer, or cheat yourself out of profits.

The first time you deal with a buyer you should ask for a money order or cashier's cheque as payment. In subsequent dealings you may feel comfortable taking a personal cheque. Auction transactions are payable in U.S. dollars, unless specified otherwise, and you may want to make that clear if this is an international transaction. The money order also has to be an international money order if this is a cross-border exchange.

Your next communication with the buyer will go something like this:

Hi Pinky,
I hope you will be pleased with this piece. Please send an international money order or cashier's cheque in US funds for $32 plus $4 shipping to:
   Sally Forth, 64 Skywalker Dr., Tatooine, Ontario, Canada
I will let you know when your payment arrives.
Thanks,
Sally

Your next step is that dreaded Internet process known as "waiting." Sellers prefer to receive their payment within five days, but this is not possible with international mail. You should wait two weeks before sending off the inevitable "have-you-sent-your-payment" query.

While you are waiting, you can package the item for shipping, if you haven't already done so. It's been my experience that there is no such thing as too much packing material for an item. Shippers are quite capable of exerting enough force to turn coal into diamonds, and you should cushion your piece for this eventuality.

When the buyer's payment arrives, there are two things a good seller does right away — e-mail the buyer that the payment has arrived, and leave him or her positive feedback on the auction site. Ask the buyer to let you know when the package arrives, and off you go to the post office to complete your transaction.

Bottom-Feeding

There's a way to sell on an auction site without paying the site a cent. I call it "bottom-feeding."

Let's say you have a collectible to sell. If you've been doing your homework, you will have already checked the auction site for listings of the same item in order to determine the extent of the competition. You find a couple of the exact same collectible listed, both with several bids on them.

Wait until the first auction ends. The moment that happens, you'll be able to look at the bidders' list. It will reveal all of the bidders' e-mail addresses and the amount they offered. Often, the second-highest bid will be just slightly below the winning bid. If the price is good, e-mail that bidder with an offer:

Hi,

I was sorry to see that you did not get the 1905 American nickel that you bid on. However, I have the exact same coin in excellent condition available for the same price as your bid. I am a dependable seller, and you can check my references on the auction site. Please let me know if you are interested.

Thanks for your attention,

Gardiner Westbound

Odds are good that the bidder will accept your offer, especially if you have a good rating on the auction site. You will have sold your item without paying a listing fee or a commission. "Bottom-feeding" works, and auction sites hate it!

One note here about timing — don't try to undercut another seller by contacting bidders before the auction ends. This is particularly slimy, and could get you booted off the auction site altogether.

Damaged Goods

In spite of your packaging prowess, it's possible that your item could be damaged en route to your buyer. He or she will quickly let you know if that's the case.

If the item was insured for damage, you should promptly refund the buyer's money, and then pursue the settlement from your end. However, you may need the piece back to prove the damage to the insurance company. If you are unsure of the buyer's reputation, refund half of the money, and hold the rest until the piece is returned.

When there is no insurance, you have no obligation as the seller to refund the payment, assuming that you did a first-rate packing job. The parcel left your hands in mint condition, and after that it's not your responsibility. However, I strongly suggest that you refund half the money on a damaged piece. That way, you both share the loss equally. This seems like the ethical thing to do, and the buyer will appreciate your honesty.

What if a buyer tells you something is damaged when it isn't, hoping to get a refund? This could happen. Check the buyer's references on the auction site. If they're good, the complaint is probably legitimate. If the buyer has a poor rating or no rating, be sure you get the piece back before you send a full or partial refund.

Dealing with Negative Feedback

Even if you do everything right, it's inevitable that someone, somewhere, sometime, will leave you negative feedback. There are many less-than-sane people going about their daily lives, perpetually misunderstanding other people's intentions, comments, or actions. You can probably think of three or four that you know right now. The world of collecting, with its often obsessive nature, draws in more than its fair share of this type of individual. Which is not to say that collectors are insane: the majority of collectors are sweet, gentle people who avidly enjoy pursuing their hobbies.

But be prepared for the day you encounter a loon. During the course of your transaction, save all your e-mail correspondence with the buyer. Don't delete them until the transaction is completed and the piece has safely arrived.

Some buyers will leave negative feedback at the drop of a hat — the parcel took too long to arrive; the shipping cost too much; the same item sold for less a week later, so you "gouged" them. Negative feedback can be very damaging, and is not to be taken lightly. You will survive one or two bad comments if you have a good track record, but it does affect the way others bid on your items. Negative comments, no matter how groundless, will scare buyers off.

Most auction sites allow sellers and buyers to respond to negative feedback by posting a rebuttal. Before you do that, try to smooth things out with the buyer. A little bit of diplomacy can go a long way. If you patch things up, ask the buyer to post the rebuttal, apologizing for his previous comment. This has far more credibility than a message from you in your own defence.

If you absolutely cannot find a common ground, you'll have to post your own explanation. Once again, a polite rebuttal to the effect of "My apologies for the slow mail delivery" is more effective than "Joe is a malcontented loser who blamed me instead of the post office." If you feel that the buyer's behaviour is really out of line, you may want to warn other sellers by posting negative feedback on his or her profile. To a large extent, an auction site, like a message board, is a "self-policing" community, and your comments may help others.

PART IV

◆

Trading

CHAPTER 10

Trading Places

As LONG AS THERE have been collectors, there has been trading. Trading is the purest form of acquisition — both parties have something the other party wants and usually no money changes hands. But the exchange is not nearly as straightforward as trading baseball cards was in Grade 6. You could be sending off a piece worth hundreds of dollars to someone whom you have never met and probably never will. There's an etiquette involved to make sure that both of you have a fair and safe trade.

Collectors can be a fickle lot. It's not unusual for them to lose their passion for a particular line. Often, after collecting for a number of years, someone will stumble across an item that he or she has never seen before, and totally fall in love with it. Suddenly a new passion is born, and the old one is up for sale or trade.

Some collectors "graduate" to a higher level of collecting. They may go from collecting resin figurines, such as Boyds Bearstones, to a porcelain line, such as Disney Classics. The jump in quality carries with it a corresponding jump in cost, often reflecting the collector's own improving financial situation.

Others may simply have duplicates of a piece they want to trade for a piece they're missing. Whatever the reason, there really is only one place to go on the Internet: a message board on a collectibles site such as Yahoo! or World Collectors Net. Auction sites are strictly for buying and selling.

A trade requires you to consider a number of factors: What is the market value of the piece you are willing to trade? What is the market value of the piece that you want? Are you willing to ante up some cash if the values aren't equal? Would you be better off selling your piece, then buying the one that you want on the secondary market? How credible is your potential trading partner? Will the trader deliver the piece as promised? Can the items be shipped with the reasonable expectation that they will both arrive undamaged?

Not quite as simple as "I'll trade you my banana for your Oreos."

We've covered message boards earlier in the book, and that's where you will post your message. For this example, you are looking to trade a Hallmark ornament of "Batman and Robin — Dynamic Duo," which was released in 1996, for the Hallmark Superman ornament, released the same year. Superman was a limited-edition piece and harder to find, so you bought two of the others, hoping to trade later. (See — you're learning!)

Before you post your message, you'd better determine the relative value of both pieces. First, you check eBay or Auctions.com, where you discover that "Dynamic Duo" is selling for around $70, while Superman is going for around $110. Then check the secondary-market listings in *Collecting Figures* magazine. The pieces are valued at $90 and $160 respectively. Now you have a sense of the price ranges involved for both pieces, and you can decide whether you want to sweeten the deal by offering another piece with "Batman" or whether you are willing to make up the difference in cash. Hopefully they will trade for "Dynamic Duo" and a lesser piece from your collection so that you won't have to spend any money. (You could even get lucky and find someone who will settle for an equal trade.)

Off you go to a Hallmark message board where you post this message:

Looking to Trade - "Dynamic Duo" + for "Superman"
I am looking to trade a mint 1996 "Dynamic Duo" for the
1996 Limited Edition "Superman." Open to negotiation.

There — you've left it wide open. Your "plus" sign in the headline indicated that you were willing to offer more than just the ornament, and "Open to negotiation" indicates that you would like to settle for an equal trade, but are willing to discuss it.

CHAPTER 11

Practise Safe Trading

The Trust Factor

As with all Internet exchanges, there's the matter of trust. How do you know that your trading partner is going to send the piece that you have agreed to trade for?

Follow the usual procedures. If your partner is an established member of the message board neighbourhood, you have little to worry about. It's still wise to ask for three references from past trading partners, and he or she should ask the same of you. Keep all your e-mail from these exchanges until the transaction is complete in case you need them later for reference.

If the pieces are roughly equivalent in size and weight, then you both pay the shipping yourselves. If one piece is much heavier, you may have to work out a deal whereby one party pays the difference in shipping charges. You should both decide on methods of shipment — courier or postal system — and agree on insurance coverage. You should both ship your items at approximately the same time, so that neither party ends up nervously waiting for days to see whether he or she has been ripped off or not.

OTHER PRECAUTIONS

If you are trading expensive limited-edition pieces, here's another method you can follow. Limited-edition pieces generally come

with a certificate of authenticity. Since the piece is greatly devalued without it, exchange the certificates first. That way, if your
partner doesn't follow through when you send the actual piece,
the piece he has failed to send you has been devalued since you
possess the certificate.

This same method can be applied to trades of multiple
pieces. Let's say that you are trading three Cherished Teddies for
two Hallmark ornaments. Send two pieces for one in the first
shipment, and then one for one in the second. If possible, hold
back the rarest piece for the second exchange. The completion
of the first exchange shows good faith on both sides, and the
second completes the deal. It will cost you more in shipping,
but it's better than losing all three pieces in a scam.

If you anticipate that the piece you are willing to trade will
increase in value and you are not in a rush to complete your collection, you may be better off to wait for a couple of years and
sell it, then buy the piece you are lusting after. The problem
with this plan, of course, is that the piece you want may escalate
in value as well, leaving you no further ahead. This method
really is a gamble.

"Domino" Trading

No, this isn't about trading dominoes, although I'm sure there
are people who do. It's about making a series of trades that lead
to the piece you actually want.

You've been collecting Lilliput Lane cottages for a number
of years, but lately you've been hankering for a Swarovski crystal sculpture to add to your collection. Swarovski crystal is very
expensive, so you've been checking the Swarovski message
boards regularly to see if you can find a bargain. Then, one day
this message appears:

Wanted to Trade - Swarovski "Pegasus" for Lladro
I am pruning my Swarovski collection to add some new
Lladro pieces, and would like to trade the 1998 Collectors'
Club piece, "Pegasus," for a retired Lladro piece of equal
value.

You would love to get "Pegasus," but don't have any Lladro
figurines to trade for it. That's where domino trading comes in.

First, e-mail the person who posted the message, and ask if
they would mind holding on to it for you for a couple of days
while you work out a deal. If they agree, then you can get to
work.

Through the usual means, determine the value of "Pegasus," which turns out to be approximately $400. Scan your Lil-
liput Lane collection for a piece of equivalent value that you are
willing to trade. You have one: the "Disney Train Station," a
limited-edition release of only 500 pieces. You like it, but you
love the Swarovski. Head for two message boards — Lilliput
Lane and Lladro — and post this message:

Looking to Trade - LE "Disney Train Station" for Lladro
I would like to trade my Lilliput Lane "Disney Train Station"
for a retired Lladro piece of similar value. This piece was
released as a Limited Edition of only 500 pieces at the
Disney Collectibles Convention in Sept. 1998, and is valued
at $400 - 500 on the secondary market.

Odds are good that someone will take you up on your offer,
either a Lilliput collector who has a Lladro they aren't enam-
oured with, or a Lladro collector who is expanding into Lilliput
Lane sculptures. You then assess the value of the Lladro being
offered and work out your deals with both parties. If you can
determine that they are both reliable traders, then there's no

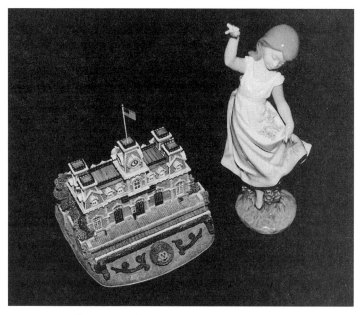

Lilliput Lane "Train Station" for Lladro piece.

need for you to ever receive the Lladro piece — just have the owner send it straight to the trader from whom you are getting the Swarovski, while you send him the Lilliput piece. Everyone is happy.

As I'm sure you've gathered, this type of trading is not for the faint of heart, but I've done it, and it works. You can even expand it so that there are four or five parties involved. However, that takes a lot of negotiating, and frankly, you'd be less frustrated playing with your real dominoes.

Cashing in on Trades

Collectors are often more interested in adding to their own collection than they are in the value of the piece they are willing to trade to achieve their goal. Sometimes you will receive an item in a trade that is worth more than the item you traded away. You could quickly turn it around and sell it in an auction, actually making money off your trade.

Savvy traders usually keep a list of collectors they have sold items to in the past. Instead of going the auction route, which can be costly and time-consuming, they may just offer the piece for sale to previous customers via e-mail. An Internet friend, with whom I had traded before, had told me that she collected Breyer horses. Breyers are nicely detailed plastic horses that have been made since the '50s. I stumbled across some in a yard sale, and bought all nine horses for $60. That afternoon, I resold the lot to my Internet friend for $120, and she subsequently resold them individually in auction for a total of $180. (Don't worry — she kept two for herself.) It pays to keep track of your contacts.

Your local flea market can also come in handy when it comes to cashing in on trades. If you can spot a trend early — it helps if you know a ten-year-old — you can stock up on a future collectible before it becomes scarce. In 1998, for example, you could have noticed the popularity of Pokémon playing cards. For $3 a package, you could have loaded up on a couple of dozen sets. By the end of 1999, when the early cards had become scarce and were selling for $6 a pack, you could make your move. You could sell them in auction individually — which is hardly worth the trouble for a $3 profit, less commission — or you could head down to the flea market.

Flea market vendors get the bulk of their stock from garage sales and real auctions. You can spot them at yard sales because they are the people who buy a large box of apparent junk for a dollar. They then go through their purchase, determining what they can resell and pricing it individually. Often they end up with items that they wouldn't normally carry and whose secondary-market values they're unsure of. Sunday morning, you show up at the flea market bright and early with a bag full of unopened

Pokémon cards. Well, they know that Pokémon is hot, and you offer to trade for a couple of their items. How about those six plastic horses there? Or maybe those two little green Pocket Dragons? Soon you've parlayed your $72 investment into $150 to $200. Sure beats the interest at the bank.

The Mercy Trade

Not unlike the mercy buy, which was discussed in Part II.

This is the only situation when an auction site can be useful when you are looking for a trade. A piece that you want is up for auction. Since the person who listed it obviously wants to sell it, there's not much you can do until the auction is over. Keep an eye on the item. If you're lucky, it won't get any bids. After the auction closes, send a note to the seller suggesting a trade. You may point out that he or she might have better luck selling the piece you are offering to trade. You may wish to suggest that you pay the listing fee on the item that didn't sell.

If this is the second or third time that the seller has failed to sell the piece, she may just take you up on your offer. The mercy trade comes to fruition, and all it cost you was a couple of bucks for her original listing.

PART V

◆

Creating
a Showcase

Building Your
Own Web Site

CHAPTER 12

Getting Started

FOR MOST PEOPLE, BUILDING a Web site is a mind-boggling proposition. But to tell you the truth, it's not that tough to create a simple Web site.

If you are a seller, the advantage of having your own Web site is that you can list and display all of your items for free. Some collectors create their own sites just to show off their personal collections, while fans of a particular line will set up a site dedicated to the object of their passion, often including self-penned histories of the line and obscure information that they've gleaned. It's fun to do, and far more engaging than television these days.

While anything related to the Internet may seem intimidating and highly technical, it's not that hard to set up a simple Web site. There are dozens of programs available that allow you to build a site simply by filling out prepackaged templates. That's the easiest route. There are also hundreds of books with detailed information on HTML, the language in which Web pages are written. If you want to delve further into the subject, buy any book written by Laura Lemay. She's the patron saint of HTML, and her books are incredibly friendly and easy to understand.

But, since you've already spent your cash on *this* book, let's tackle the mountain together. We're going to build a very simple

Web site for selling collectibles — Cherished Teddies, in fact. Grab the coffee!

The Drawing Board

In the immortal words of Julie Andrews, "Let's start at the very beginning..."

Your first task is defiantly low-tech: get out a pencil and paper and plan what the site will look like. Sketch the layout of the opening page. What text do you want on it? Do you want pictures? Do you want links to other pages? Do you want viewers to be able to e-mail you? Do you want it to have a specific background? Consider all of those possibilities, list your preferences, and then draw away.

For this page, we want a title at the top that says "Biff's Cherished Teddies." We want a list of pieces for sale, with photos and prices. We'll skip the picture "wallpaper" background because it takes too long to load; instead we may go for a coloured background instead. We will link to a second page where we can list related Cherished Teddies' items. And we definitely want an e-mail option, so that viewers can contact us.

After the sketch is done, we return to the computer to turn our "vision" into reality.

Doing It the Hard Way

We'll cheat later, but for now we are going to actually start from scratch and write the page in HTML code. On your computer, find the simplest text editor you've got. Windows comes with Notepad, and you can't get much more basic than that. Macintosh computers come with the aptly-named SimpleText. That's where we'll start.

You may notice that all Web pages have approximately the same layout. They have a title, and a main section, and paragraphs. HTML just clarifies what these sections are so that a browser, such as Netscape Navigator or Internet Explorer, can display them. Working in the text editor, we break the page down into its component parts, using basic HTML "tags." Tags are the instructions that the browser needs for translation, and are always surrounded by angle brackets. Any writing that is in parentheses will not appear on a browser.

Start with this tag:

<HTML>

This tells the browser that it is receiving a page written in HTML.

Next comes this tag:

<HEAD>

This will contain the heading that appears in the bar at the top edge of the browser window; this text won't appear on the page.

Then we add the title tag:

<TITLE>Biff's Cherished Teddies

That will appear on the same bar where your little exit "X" is.

Now, this is where everyone — me included — starts to make the same mistake. We all forget to "close" our tags. The browser doesn't know when the title ends unless we tell it, so you have to close the tag by placing a forward slash in front of it.

<TITLE>Biff's Cherished Teddies</TITLE>

And since this is the end of the heading, you also have to close it.

</HEAD>

So far, so good. Now we get to the actual page. This is what will appear in the browser window, and it is called the "body."

<BODY>

Those anatomy courses are really paying off now! We start here with the title we want at the top of the page. And wouldn't you know it, there's just such a tag for this occasion. There are actually three tags to choose from — <H1>, <H2>, and <H3> — and they create titles in big, bigger, and biggest sizes. Very splashy. For now, we'll show a bit of decorum and use the smallest:

<H1>Biff's Cherished Teddies</H1>

(Remember to close the tag!)

For now, let's pause and see how the page is coming along. Close the document off with these commands:

</BODY></HTML>

Your text editor document should look like this:

<HTML>

<HEAD>

<TITLE>Biff's Cherished Teddies</TITLE>

</HEAD>

<BODY>

<H1>Biff's Cherished Teddies</H1>

</BODY>

</HTML>

Not very appealing, I know, but it gets better. Save this file to a Temporary folder somewhere, but save it as an HTML file, *not* a text file. We'll call it biff.html (your program may drop the "l" and just add the extension "htm" — don't panic, it still works).

Start your browser, click on *File* on the menu bar, find biff.html and open it in the browser. You should see the image on the following page.

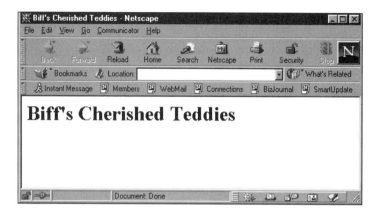

That's it. You won't see any of the other codes that you've entered. And the bar at the top should have the same title. If it didn't work, and you're seeing all of the text that you typed instead of just the title, then you didn't save your file with the HTML extension. If you are seeing nothing at all, then you probably haven't closed one of your tags.

In case you are wondering, you don't have to type your HTML tags in capital letters. It just makes them easier to see when you're editing.

LOVE YOUR BODY!

You now have the basic structure for your whole Web page. We just have to fill in the body. We'll do the text first, and leave the photos for later, since they're a bit more complicated.

We're going to list four Cherished Teddies. The first one is "Nina." You need to make a space between the title — "Biff's Cherished Teddies" — and your items, so we'll use the "paragraph" command <P>:

<P>Nina - 1997 National Event Figurine - $30</P>

As you can see, you don't need to leave a space after a command, in this case <P>, since the browser won't display your commands. Now your text editor looks like this:

```
<HTML>
<HEAD>
<TITLE>Biff's Cherished Teddies</TITLE>
</HEAD>
<BODY>
<H1>Biff's Cherished Teddies</H1>
<P>Nina - 1997 National Event Figurine - $30</P>
</BODY>
</HTML>
```

We haven't specified a "font size," so the browser will automatically choose "font size=+0," the standard font size on most sites. However, since you are trying to sell some items, you probably want to strengthen your presentation by using a larger font:

```
<P><FONT SIZE=+1>Nina - 1997 National Event Figurine -
  $30</FONT></P>
```

You will notice I've closed the font and paragraph tags in the reverse order that I laid them down. This isn't essential, but some browsers crash when they receive commands out of order, so it's a good habit to maintain.

Finally, we'll want to make the word "Nina" stand out from the rest of the line. There are several options for doing that, and we'll use the easiest, "bold" <B>:

```
<P><FONT SIZE=+1><B>Nina</B> - 1997 National Event
  Figurine - $30</FONT></P>
```

Note that we "closed" the "bold" at the end of the word we want to emphasize. You could also have used "italics" <I></I> or a different font colour:

```
<FONT COLOR=RED></FONT>
```

Having conquered the first line, we carry on and add three more bears using the same commands:

```
<P><FONT SIZE=+1><B>Harrison</B> - Retired 1996 -
  $25</FONT></P>
```

```
<P><FONT SIZE=+1><B>Preston</B> - Canadian
  Exclusive - $50</FONT></P>
```

```
<P><FONT SIZE=+1><B>Humphrey</B> - 1998 Regional
  Event - $60</FONT></P>
```

Here's the completed code for the whole page:

```
<HTML>
<HEAD>
<TITLE>Biff's Cherished Teddies</TITLE>
</HEAD>
<BODY>
<H1>Biff's Cherished Teddies</H1>
<P><FONT SIZE=+1><B>Nina</B> - 1997 National Event
  Figurine - $30</FONT></P>
<P><FONT SIZE=+1><B>Harrison</B> - Retired 1996 -
  $25</FONT></P>
<P><FONT SIZE=+1><B>Preston</B> - Canadian
  Exclusive - $50</FONT></P>
<P><FONT SIZE=+1><B>Humphrey</B> - 1998 Regional
  Event - $60</FONT></P>
</BODY>
</HTML>
```

Now, resave the file, as biff.html, to your Temporary folder, and let's take a look at it in the browser:

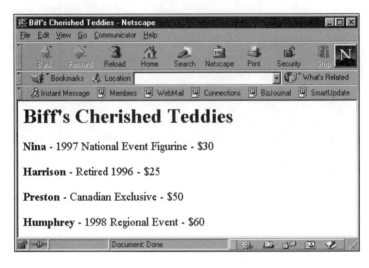

So far so good, but how are they going to contact you if they want to buy something? That's where the "mailto" command comes in handy.

Return to the text editor. At the end of the body, *before* you close it, add this line (with your e-mail address):

```
<P><FONT SIZE=+1>Contact <A HREF=
  "mailto:biff@acme.net">Biff Capon</A> </FONT></P>
```

When anyone clicks on your e-mail address — which is now a "link" — a little mail window will open and they can type a message and send it to you. Very cool.

Notice in that last bit the command <A HREF=>, closed by </A>. This is an indispensable command. <A> is an "anchor," and when a viewer clicks on it, it tells the browser to jump somewhere else. <HREF>, if you care to know, stands for "hypertext reference." The <HREF> is usually a URL, or Web address, for another page or location. We'll run into this again later, so keep it in mind.

CHAPTER 13

Getting Fancy

So far we are conveying information, but we're definitely not going to win any points for style. By adding some simple commands we can spruce things up a bit.

First off, it will look good if the heading is centred on the page. Add the <CENTER> command to the heading line, and close it:

```
<H1><CENTER>Biff's Cherished Teddies</CENTER></H1>
```

And wouldn't it be lovely if there were one of those nice embossed horizontal lines between the heading and the pieces for sale? There's a tag for that — <HR> — and you *don't* close this one since it isn't actually a command, it's just a thingy that sits there:

```
<H1><CENTER>Biff's Cherished Teddies</CENTER></H1>
<HR>
```

Let's centre the last line, the one with the "mailto" address, just to balance things off. Here's the code for the page up to this point, followed by the way it looks in Netscape:

```
<HTML>
<HEAD>
<TITLE>Biff's Cherished Teddies</TITLE>
</HEAD>
<BODY>
```

```
<H1><CENTER>Biff's Cherished Teddies</CENTER></H1>
<HR>
<P><FONT SIZE=+1><B>Nina</B> - 1997 National Event
  Figurine - $30</FONT></P>
<P><FONT SIZE=+1><B>Harrison</B> - Retired 1996 -
  $25</FONT></P>
<P><FONT SIZE=+1><B>Preston</B> - Canadian
  Exclusive - $50</FONT></P>
<P><FONT SIZE=+1><B>Humphrey</B> - 1998 Regional
  Event - $60</FONT></P>
<P><CENTER><FONT SIZE=+1>Contact <A HREF=
  "mailto:biff@acme.net">Biff Capon</A></FONT>
  </CENTER></P>
</BODY>
</HTML>
```

Biff's Cherished Teddies

Nina - 1997 National Event Figurine - $30

Harrison - Retired 1996 - $25

Preston - Canadian Exclusive - $50

Humphrey - 1998 Regional Event - $60

Contact <u>Biff Capon</u>

We planned to add a coloured background to the page, and this is the time to do it. This is where HTML takes a turn for the complicated. The founding mothers and fathers of HTML apparently used up all their easy-to-remember names on tags for text. When it came to colours, they really fell apart.

Most browsers will accept the basic colour commands —

<RED>, <YELLOW>,<BLUE>, <GREEN>, <PURPLE>, etc. — and give you those standard colours as a font or as a background. However, the many *shades* of those colours are written as "hexadecimal" values. For example, dark red is listed as "#8B0000." You can find charts for colour values all over the Web, or, if you see a colour you like on another Web page, just look at the "Page source" under your "View" menu on the browser. It will show you the value for that colour. Here's a few in case you want to experiment:

Aqua	"#00FFFF"
Dark Blue	"#00008B"
Grey	"#808080"
Hot Pink	"#FF69B4"
Magenta	"#FF00FF"
Light Green	"#90EE90"
Orchid	"#DA70D6"
Tan	"#D2B48C"
White	"#FFFFFF"
Black	"#000000"

There are dozens of these "hex triplets," as they are known, and unless you've got a lot of spare time on your hands there's no point trying to memorize them. Find a chart.

The background colour we'll use is Sea Green — "#2E8B57."

The tag for a background colour fits into the same parentheses as the <BODY> tag. On our page, it will be indicated this way:
<BODY BGCOLOR="#2E8B57">

You will note that <BGCOLOR> is always followed by an equal sign, and that hex triplets always start with a pound or number sign, and are enclosed in quotation marks.

Now that our background is a lovely sea-green colour, we may want to change our text from black to something more stylish, such as dark blue. (Be careful with your colour combinations.

For instance, red text over a black background can be very hard to read.) The tag for changing the text colour from its default colour — black — goes into the same parentheses as <BODY> and <BGCOLOR>.

```
<BODY BGCOLOR="#2E8B57" TEXT="#00008B">
```

You don't have to close these colours at the end. When you close </BODY>, that will end them. Here's the code for the page, with everything we've covered so far:

```
<HTML>
<HEAD>
<TITLE>Biff's Cherished Teddies</TITLE>
</HEAD>
<BODY BGCOLOR="#2E8B57" TEXT="#00008B">
<H1><CENTER>Biff's Cherished Teddies</CENTER></H1>
<HR>
<P><FONT SIZE=+1><B>Nina</B> - 1997 National Event
   Figurine - $30</FONT></P>
<P><FONT SIZE=+1><B>Harrison</B> - Retired 1996 -
   $25</FONT></P>
<P><FONT SIZE=+1><B>Preston</B> - Canadian
   Exclusive - $50</FONT></P>
<P><FONT SIZE=+1><B>Humphrey</B> - 1998 Regional
   Event - $60</FONT></P>
<P><CENTER><FONT SIZE=+1>Contact <A HREF=
   "mailto:biff@acme.net">Biff Capon</A> </FONT>
   </CENTER></P>
</BODY>
</HTML>
```

Next, we cheat. There are ways to get the same result without having to juggle HTML commands or remember to close the tags. In the next chapter we'll explore one method.

CHAPTER 14

Doing It
the Easy Way

CONGRATULATIONS! YOU MADE IT through HTML boot camp. Like all boot camp experiences, HTML programming is designed to make you wish you had never been born. After it's over, you realize that life is beautiful, and that there are ways to cut corners. At least now you have a very basic concept of how HTML works. In this chapter we'll be dealing with an HTML editor — specifically, Netscape Composer, which comes with the full version of Netscape Communicator and is one of the most common HTML editing programs around. There are, however, hundreds to choose from.

With Composer, you start with a blank, white HTML page. You enter the text that you want to see, just as you would on any word processing program. All you have to do is centre your heading, add bold to your words you want to emphasize, alter your font sizes, and choose a coloured background from the palette in the menu bar. Composer adds all of the HTML tags for you. Ain't life grand! At this point, if you do decide to get fancy with your newly acquired knowledge of HTML, you can actually go into the HTML version of the page, revealing all the tags, and muck about. Just select "Edit HTML" from the Tools menu, and voilà. Impress your friends, or at the very least, your cat.

Using the HTML editor is the easiest way to add graphics to your page, because you are going to be dealing with "tables."

A table is a grid of rows and columns that places your text and graphics on the page. You can vary the number of rows and columns, as well as the width of the table. The individual boxes of a table are called cells, which will be familiar if you've used a spreadsheet program.

We're going to redo "Biff's Cherished Teddies" page, using Composer and incorporating a table.

Start with a blank HTML page. Centre your cursor, select "Heading 1" from the font style menu at the top of the page, and type in your heading, "Biff's Cherished Teddies."

For the next row, find that little "Line" icon at the top of the page, and select it. It "draws" an embossed, horizontal line.

Now we're going to start a table. There's an icon at the top that looks like a grid. (On the current version of Composer, it actually says "Table," a dead giveaway.) Click on it.

Another menu will open. It will ask you for number of rows and columns. You have four Cherished Teddies to list, and four photos, so that's four rows and two columns.

You can choose to centre your table on the page. It will ask you for "Border line width," which refers to the lines on the grid, and it defaults to one pixel if you don't change it. One pixel is fine. "Cell spacing" refers to the space between cells and it defaults to one pixel, which is also fine. "Cell padding" denotes the space between what is inside the cell and the edge of the cell. I usually select 5 pixels, so the cells don't look too crammed. (It may also refer to the psychiatric facility you'll be in after working with HTML!)

You can change the width and height of the table, but for this exercise just leave it at 100 percent. Some menus will default to "Columns of equal width." Turn this off, or you'll get a very strange-looking page. You also have the option of giving your table a different-coloured background than the rest of the page. We'll pass on this, but you can experiment with it later if you like.

Here's the Composer table menu, with all of the above selections made:

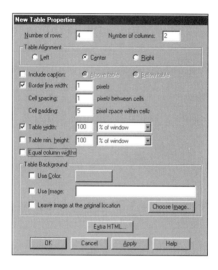

After you've made your selections, click on "OK," or press the Enter key, and the table will appear on your page:

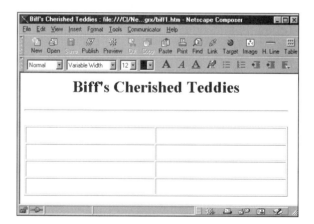

Now type the names of your four Cherished Teddies in the right-hand column, one Teddy per cell. You can format the fonts as you enter them, making the names bold by selecting the

"Bold" icon from the menu bar. The centre line of the grid will move to the left as you type, but don't worry about it. All will become clear later.

Next, we add photos to the left-hand cells. You have shots of all four figurines, and I recommend resizing them all so they're 60 pixels wide. The smaller you make them, the faster they will load, and the less likely you are to lose a potential customer. Generally, a 60-pixel width is large enough to see a figurine. (If you are selling Picasso's "Guernica," ignore this.)

Park your cursor in the top left-hand cell. In the menu bar, you will find an "Image" icon, or a drop-down menu under "Insert" that includes "Image" on it. Click on either of these, and another dialogue box will open. It will prompt you for the name of the image, and you can hit "Browse" and look for it in your files. After you've found it, double-click on the name of the image. That closes the "Browse" box, and adds the name to your dialogue box. Just hit the "OK" button, and the photo will appear in your top left cell. You may have to centre it by using the "Center" button in the menu. Repeat this for the other three photos, and you will end up with a page that looks like this:

Now, here's the amazing part. You can "hide" the table's borders so that you end up with a very clean-looking page. Put your cursor in any of the cells, and click on your *right* mouse button. (If you don't have a two-button mouse, select "Table Properties" from the menu bar.) You'll get the "Table properties" dialogue box again. Change the "Border width" from 1 pixel to zero and hit Enter. Here's what you end up with:

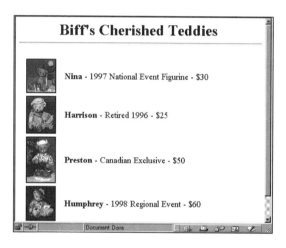

Elegant in its simplicity, as Lucretius used to say.

All you have left to do is add the contact link at the bottom of the page, beneath the table. Type in "Contact Biff Capon," and then highlight it with the cursor. In the menu at the top of the page you'll find an icon for "Link" — it may be in a drop-down menu. Clicking on it will give you a dialogue box for Links. In the space provided, just enter the "mailto" command, as discussed earlier — "mailto:biff@acme.com." When you close the box, your last highlighted sentence or words will now be identified as a link. So when a potential customer clicks on the "Contact Biff Capon" section, an e-mail box will open and they can send Biff a message. Save this page as in your Temporary folder, and let's move on to Page 2.

Linking to Other Pages

One truly amazing aspect of the Internet is the ability to use links to jump from one page to another instantly. For the type of page you've created, links from the photos will come in handy. Often a page like this will have small "thumbnails" of the items, which the viewer can click to see a larger version of the photo. You can do this by creating four separate pages, placing a larger version of the image on each page, then making the small thumbnail images into links. Let's start with Nina.

Using a new blank HTML page in Composer, put the same centred heading at the top of this page — "Biff's Cherished Teddies" — that you used on the last page. Under it, insert your larger image of Nina, following the same method we used to place the smaller photos. This image will have to have a different name, such as "nina2.jpg," or else you'll end up with the tiny thumbnail on this page, too. You may want to add some text under the photo, such as "Nina – 1997 National Event Figurine." That's it. Your second page is done.

Save this page as "biff2.html," and then carry on with your three pages for the other three bears. Save them as "biff3.html," "biff4.html," and "biff5html." Without doing anything too fancy, you're actually creating your own small, multipage Web site.

Once you've finished all of your pages, go back to the first page, "biff1.html." Now you're going to add links that lead to the other pages. Park your cursor on the first "thumbnail" of Nina by clicking on it. Again select "Link" from the top icons, or find "Add link" in one of your drop-down menus. Open the "Link" dialogue box, and, in the space provided, type in "biff2.html." Close the dialogue box by hitting Enter, and now your little photo of Nina is a link to the larger version.

Repeat for the other three "thumbnails." You won't be able to test the links to see whether they are working from within the HTML editor. You will have to save "biff1.html" after you've added your links, and then test them using your Web browser. As long as all of your pages are in the Temp folder together, all the links should work. Now you need to upload your entire Web site so others can access it.

CHAPTER 15

Uploading Your Site

Next comes the hardest thing, I think, to understand about HTML pages. Even though you are seeing photos of Cherished Teddies on your pages, those photos are not embedded on the pages. They are really still in your Temp folder with "biff1.html," "biff2.html," etc., and your browser is following a path to where the images are and calling them up so you can see them.

When you look at a photo in a magazine, it's on the same page as the article you're reading. To get the idea of how pictures are related to HTML pages, pretend that you're reading an article where holes have been cut out for the photos, and the photos are on the next page. You can still see them through the holes, but they are not with the text. When you inserted your "thumbnails" into the table, the HTML editor put in a code to call up the photos. If you open "biff1.html" with your browser, then use the "Page source" command under the View menu, you'll find this code where your pictures are supposed to be: <IMG SRC="nina1.jpg">, <IMG SRC="harrison1.jpg">, etc.

<IMG SRC> is the command for calling up a graphic or photo. You will need to know this.

Before you can upload your brand new Web site, you need a place to upload it to! We discussed this earlier in the chapter on "Selling," but here's a recap:

Most Internet service providers (ISPs) allow you some space on their server where you can store Web pages. If your ISP doesn't provide any free room, there are two generous servers that will — Angelfire (www.angelfire.com), and Geocities (www.geocities.com).

Both sites give you clear instructions about setting up your space, or directory. You will be asked to choose an area where you want your directory to be — for instance, hobbies, sports, your state, a fictional neighbourhood, etc. Then you will be asked to name your own directory.

For the Biff example, we go to Angelfire, set up a directory in the Nebraska section (nb), and call the site bct, for "biff's cherished teddies." (It's a good idea to keep everything lower-case, since it's easier to type and people will be less prone to make mistakes when they enter the URL.) The URL address for our Web site will be http://www.angelfire.com/nb/bct.

After we register, Angelfire automatically sends us a password so that we can upload to our site. We return to the Angelfire home page, and select "Login." Here there are two blanks to fill in — the directory name, and the password. Since we're already at Angelfire, we don't have to type in that part of the URL. We only have to key in /nb/bct then the password, and hit "Submit."

We arrive at a page called a "Web Shell." It has plenty of stylish buttons on it; the one we want is "Browse."

Clicking the Browse button will open up a little window that shows all the files on your computer. Go to the Temp folder, and find "biff1.html." Double-click on it. The window closes, and "biff1.html" is sitting in the dialogue box at the bottom of the Web shell page. Hit "Upload," and away it goes! As if by magic, Angelfire's server copies the page from your computer to the "bct" directory we set up. It will appear in your list of files right above the Upload button.

Now, remember what I mentioned about the pictures — they're not actually on the page you just uploaded. Only the code giving the name and location of the pictures is there. You have to upload the photos individually.

This works the same way as uploading the pages did. Hit Browse again, and find "nina1.jpg," your "thumbnail" for Nina. Double-click on it. The window closes. Hit Upload. The server does its thing. Carry on like that, uploading all five html files for the bears, and all of the photos, small and large versions. When you are done, your file list will look like this:

biff1.html

biff2.html

biff3.html

biff4.html

biff5.html

nina1.jpg

nina2.jpg

harrison1.jpg

harrison2.jpg

preston1.jpg

preston2.jpg

humphrey1.jpg

humphrey2.jpg

You didn't know you'd done all that work, did you? Well, we're not done yet.

Making Photos and Links Work on the Web Site

You've tested your links, and they all worked — the pictures all appeared. But now that you've uploaded everything, that's irrelevant.

They may have worked on your home computer, where the

browser knew to look for everything in the Temp folder on your hard drive. But now your pages have moved to foreign territory, and codes have to be altered to account for that fact.

Internet servers store all of the graphics that are uploaded as "Images," and that is where your photos have ended up — in an "Images" folder that the server created for you. You will have to go into the HTML code on your pages and revise them. Don't be scared — it's fairly simple.

Highlight the first HTML file in your list, "biff1.html." Then select the "Edit" button.

You'll see the HTML code for the page "biff1.html." (Of course, you're an old hand at this by now.) Find the first <IMG SRC> for Nina. It will still say <IMG SRC="nina1.jpg">. Add the correct location of the photo, changing the command so it reads <IMG SRC="/nb/bct/images/nina1.jpg">. Do the same for all the photos and you're back in business!

Now it's time to fix the links from the thumbnails to the pages with the larger pictures. Earlier, I mentioned that the <A HREF> command was one of the most important commands. It is the command for links, and when you added links to the thumbnails, the HTML editor was inserting that code for you. If you look at the code for "biff1.html," you would find this code on your small photo of Nina: <A HREF="biff2.html">. That's the link to your second page, which worked fine at home. Here you have to add the directory to it: <A HREF= "/nb/bct/biff2.html">.

Go ahead and add that prefix — /nb/bct/ — to all of the links from the thumbnails. You don't have to alter the "Contact Biff Capon" link. It's an e-mail link, and will work just fine.

When you're done, save the page, then go into the other four HTML pages that you've uploaded, and fix the <IMG SRC> commands by adding the prefix /nb/bct/images/.

The fact of the matter is that you could have done all this

when you first created the pages. But you wouldn't have been able to test the links or see the photos on your own computer, because all the code references would have been to Angelfire.

After you've made your alterations and saved your changes, it's time to check out the site. Go to your home page — http://www.angelfire.com/nb/bct/biff1.html — and click away. All the thumbnails should be there, and they should all link up to the large-version pages. Use your browser's "Back" button to get back to your home page. Send Biff an e-mail, and say Hi for me.

Congratulations! You've created your own Web site, albeit a small and very simple one. We've just scratched the surface of the amazing things that you can do on a Web site, and I suggest you buy a book on HTML if you want to discover more.

PROMOTING YOUR NEW WEB SITE

Now that you've become a Webmaster, there's the problem of getting noticed on the World Wide Web. Your most inexpensive advertising tool is only an auction away! Every time you list an item for auction, include your Web site's URL in the item description. (Biff Capon would have entered http://www.angelfire.com/nb/bct/biff1.html). For the cost of the listing fee — between 50 cents and two dollars — the entire planet can find your site. Another promotional tool is "Add Me," at www.add-me.com. Through this site, you can add yourself to dozens of Internet search engines, and the best part is it's free!

A Career in Auctions

YOU'VE NO DOUBT HEARD stories of people who've packed in their regular jobs and started to make a living by trading on auction sites from their homes. I'm sure this is possible, but it would take a lot of savvy and a lot of luck. You can acquire savvy, but luck is generally in short supply, which is why I definitely do not recommend this course of action. Keep your day job, and leave your time online as playtime. If you are absolutely determined to make a go of it, here's my list of pointers for serious auctioneers:

If you can't double what you paid for something, it's not worth selling ◆ Think about the amount of work involved in selling just one piece. First of all, you had to find and buy it. That's time and money you could have spent some other way. Then, after you sell it, you have to take the time to find packing materials, package the item properly, go to the post office, go to the bank to cash the payment, and keep up your e-mail correspondence with the buyer until the transaction is complete. Unless you make a good return on your investment, you'll end up working for minimum wage.

Don't stick to one collectible. Sell a variety of items ◆ If you put all your eggs in one basket, like those poor souls who invested heavily in Beanie Babies, you'll soon be out cleaning washrooms for a living. (Not that there's anything wrong with that...) Sell all sorts of items, even those you don't know anything about. As long as you can get them for a good price, you'll snag a few surprises, and learn a lot along the way.

Don't hold out for prices to go higher. Sell while you can ◆ In the summer of 1999, Harmony Kingdom released a limited-edition piece called "Disorderly Eating" that was only available in England. A friend kindly picked one up for me for $75. The edition was quickly sold out, and within a couple of weeks "Disorderly Eating" turned up on eBay, selling for $800! Avid collectors in the States were snapping them up at outrageous prices. I couldn't believe my good fortune, and decided to wait a little to see how high the price would go. Well, two weeks later, it was selling for $400. That's because the heavy hitters with money had all made their purchases. By this point the market was down to the second-tier collectors. Two weeks later, "Disorderly Eating" was selling for $175. By the time this book comes out, it should be down to $75!

I still have mine, but I learned an expensive lesson. Get rid of it while the gettin' is good.

Don't use reserves ◆ Being a cautious person, this is hard for me to recommend. But I've seen it happen again and again: items with no reserve get more bids and higher final prices. It's a gamble, and you have to be prepared to lose once in a while, but people who use this approach generally come out on top.

Buy collections. Sell individual pieces ◆ Invariably, you can buy an entire collection for less than the sum of its parts. You will always make money if you go to the trouble of splitting it up and reselling each piece individually. This is how flea market dealers make a living: they buy boxes full of apparent junk from auctions or garage sales for next to nothing. Then they split up the contents and resell the individual items for a profit.

Base your success on an overview, not on each sale ◆ Notwithstanding what I said about "doubling your investment," you will lose money on some pieces and make money on others. As long as you double your *entire* investment, don't sweat the individual losses.

Buy a digital camera ◆ In an auction, a picture is everything. A clear, sharp picture of the actual item up for sale sells it far more effectively than your verbal description ever will. And digital cameras produce sharper, clearer pictures than a scan of a conventional photograph will ever provide.

Think of yourself as a store. Courtesy, integrity, and service keeps them coming back ◆ If you are doing this for a living, then you are running a virtual store. If you have items in different categories up for sale constantly, people will become familiar with your name — in fact, they will start to seek you out to see what sorts of interesting things you are offering each week. Be scrupulously honest in your dealings with customers, always keeping them informed of the status of their payments and shipments. You're running a business and should behave in a businesslike manner. Treat your clients with respect and they'll be back for more.

Stock your "store" wisely ◆ Don't bother looking for bargains in big-city flea markets. These vendors are too sophisticated to let anything of value slip through their professional fingers. You're better off hitting small-town flea markets and junk shops for some inexpensive finds. If you're in a city, yard sales are the last great frontier of unbelievable bargains. Next to them are pawn shops, which generally lag far behind the secondary market in terms of prices on collectibles. If you're in a rural area, estate auction sales are your best bet for bargains. Among the tractors and bundles of blankets you're bound to find some cranberry glass or other second-hand treasures.

Sell multiples by contacting the losing bidders ♦ When you put a piece up for auction, try to have a couple more copies of it on hand. As soon as the auction ends, contact the second- and third-highest bidders and ask if they are interested in buying. If their bids aren't significantly lower than the winning bid, you can offer it to them for their original bids. Remember, you won't be paying a listing fee or commission on these secondary sales, so it's worth it to give them a discount.

Don't add too many graphics to your listing ♦ Long loading times are the kiss of death in an online auction. Bidders are out for a thrill, not a few minutes of quiet contemplation. Avoid animation, silly sounds, movies, or mind-blowing, time-consuming graphics. One medium-size photo will do nicely, thank you.

Set up a merchant account so you can accept credit cards ♦ Nothing says legitimacy like the ability to accept credit card orders. Since many people bid on impulse, being able to charge it will make them bid sooner and higher.

Keep your opening bid low ♦ A low opening bid will get the ball rolling early and draw the attention of other bidders. But, depending on the item that you're selling, don't start out too low or bidders will think there's something wrong with your product. Starting a Ming vase at 99 cents is just an insult to the bidder's intelligence.

Don't try to sell an item when there are dozens of other copies already listed ◆ Before you put your item up, check to see how stiff the competition is. If it's heavy, hold off until the playing field opens up, or head to another auction site. Otherwise you'll drown in a sea of low prices.

Spelling, pleez! ◆ Please watch your spelling, especially in the headline for the item. Nothing does more to make you look low-class and, by association, undependable than bad spelling.

Always link to your own Web site ◆ Since this is your full-time business, you undoubtedly have your own small Web site by now. Make sure that you link to it on every item you put up for auction. It's excellent exposure for a very small price, and you'd much rather sell your collectibles with no listing fee or commission from your *own* site.

If you have a "hot" item, keep the auction short ◆ As with my example of the Harmony Kingdom piece, when you have an item that buyers are going wacky for, don't give them time to think about it. Keep the auction as short as you possibly can — three days, or even just one day if the site will let you.

Get weird! ◆ Pick up those weird things — like secret UFO tapes or dogs made out of horseshoes — that nobody in their right mind would ever want. You can find junk like this selling for a quarter at flea markets and yard sales. Someone somewhere will pay you $10 for it, and you'll have a tidy profit and a good laugh.

Try, try again ◆ Don't give up on an item just because it didn't attract any bids. Maybe the planets weren't aligned properly. Try it again, maybe in a different category. I've had items that took three tries to sell, but eventually they did. Even if they don't, one of your friends will get a lovely birthday present!

Be a buyer, too ◆ Don't forget that there's more than one way to use an auction site. Keep your eye out for bargains that you can resell. Make your purchases very early in the morning, while everyone else is still dreaming about auctions. Then sell it to them after they wake up.

Always check your buyers' feedback ◆ There's no lack of undependable buyers out there, the kind who'll wait a month to mail their payment, if they do at all. Always check their feedback, and if there are several negative comments there, send an e-mail asking for an explanation. Give them a deadline by which you expect their payment, and if it's not forthcoming, cancel the transaction. Leave them negative feedback, and ask the auction site to reimburse your commission fee. If you have "just cause," they usually will.

Keep on top of trends ◆ Check the categories page on the auction site regularly, and watch for a rising number of auctions listed in various categories. For example, "Just the Right Shoe" — a small, resin shoe figurine — may have had 53 items up for auction in June 1999, and 206 by August. That's a trend, and you will want to study it up close to see which items are listed and what they are going for. Visit the "Just the Right Shoe" Web site and bone up on the line and the retired pieces. Then, get yourself to some small-town retail outlets to buy up retired "Just the Right Shoe" sculptures before someone else beats you to them.

Gulliver's Collectibles

I hope that this book has given you some insights and some techniques to help your hobby flourish in the new millennium. Just remember the golden rule — "Buy it because you love it" — and you'll never go wrong.

Obviously I couldn't publish a book on the Internet without having a Web site to complement it, so please drop on by: **www.gulliverscollectibles.com.** You'll find some special treats there that will only be available to readers of this book. By using a rotating password taken from the text of this book, you'll be able to access exclusive secondary-market price lists, updates on trends, reviews of Web sites, and other nifty things to enhance your collecting experience. So come on by and say Hi!

Collectibles Companies Web Sites

ARMANI
http://www.the-society.com/home.html
Company: Florence Sculture d'Arte — Italy
High-end porcelain figurines, primarily of elegant women, made by Giuseppe Armani. This is the official North American site. My favourite Armani pieces are his Disney characters, which capture the spirit of the cartoons far better than his rival (Lladro's) versions.
Site Features: Info on current catalogue • Join collectors' club online • List of retired pieces with photos • Company history

ARTESANIA RINCONADA
http://www.rinconada.com
Company: Artesania Rinconada — Uruguay
Spanish and South American influences combine in exotic ceramic animal figurines. Created by twin brothers Jesus and Javier Carbajales, this charming line is finally getting the attention it deserves after 26 years in production. Expect the early retired pieces to soar in value.
Site Features: Site is U.S. distributor • Info on catalogue

BARBIE
http://www.barbie.com
Company: Mattel, Inc. — U.S.
Classic fashion doll with a huge following, in spite of Ken. Pastel-coloured site offers fans a well-stocked store with current upscale Barbies by Bob Mackie and Vera Wang. Bring your credit card.
Site Features: Official Barbie site • News • Info on current catalogue • Online shopping

BEANIE BABIES & BUDDIES
http://www.ty.com
Company: Ty, Inc. — U.S.
Those cuddly beanbag critters and their friends started a revolution in Internet collecting. Big and very slow to load — bring lunch.
Site Features: Official Ty site • News • Info on complete catalogue • Games

BESWICK
http://www.royal-doulton.com/brands_beswick.html
Company: Royal Doulton — U.K.
Classic porcelain animal figurines. Beswick has been in business since 1894, and is famous for its sculptures based on Beatrix Potter and "The Adventures of Rupert Bear."
Site Features: Info on current catalogue • Company history

BOYDS BEARS AND FRIENDS
www.boydscollectibles.com
Company: Boyds Collection Ltd. — U.S.
Humorous resin and plush bears and various other critters. Gary Lowenthal started this business out of his antique shop in Boyds, Maryland. Known as the "Head Bean," Lowenthal's irreverent sense of humour defines the line. The collectors club is called FoB — Friends of Boyds — and you can join it online.
Site Features: Info on current catalogue • News • Join collectors club

BUNNYKINS
http://www.royal-doulton.co.uk
Company: Royal Doulton — U.K.
Ceramic bunny figurines at work and play. Didn't we all have a
Bunnykins bowl when we were babies?
Site Features: Info on current catalogue

CAITHNESS GLASS
http://www.caithnessglass.co.uk
Company: Royal Doulton — U.K.
Caithness Glass in Scotland is one of the finest designers of
paperweights in the world. Colin Terris and his crew create
spectacular limited-edition pieces, some of them in runs of as
small as 35 duplicates. Beautiful site may convert you to a
paperweight collector.
Site Features: Info on catalogue • News

CALICO KITTENS
http://www.calicokittens.com
Company: Enesco Corp. — U.S.
Resin kitty cats. 'Nuff said.
Site Features: Info on current catalogue • News

CARDEW TEAPOTS
http://www.cardewdesign.com
Company: Cardew Design — U.K.
Traditional and delightfully wacky teapots from the brilliant
Paul Cardew. Cardew teapots have excellent investment
potential. Great site.
Site Features: Info on complete catalogue • News • Games
(including paint-your-own teapot!)

CHARMING TAILS
http://www.charmingtails.com
Company: Fitz and Floyd — U.S.
Woodland critter figurines by Dean Griff.
Site Features: Under construction at time of publication.

CHERISHED TEDDIES
http://www.enesco.com
Company: Enesco Corp. — U.S.
Cute resin teddy bear figurines created by Priscilla Hillman. I
thought this collectible was past its prime, but Enesco has made
some good marketing moves to push CTs back to the top.
Site Features: Info on catalogue • News
• Join collectors' club online

COALPORT
http://www.wedgwood.co.uk
Company: Wedgwood — U.K.
Distinguished British makers of figurines and tableware.
Site Features: Wedgwood site is lovely, but I can't find any
reference to Coalport.

COCA-COLA
http://www.coca-cola.com
Company: The Coca-Cola Company — U.S.
Doc Pemberton's "pick-me-up" is still going strong over a
century after its invention. There are millions of Coke
collectors around the world, and this very hip site is updated
regularly with new features to keep them coming back.
A great site!
Site Features: Info on catalogue • Games • Online store
• Message board

COLLECTIBLE WORLD STUDIOS
http://www.collectibleworld.com/index.html
Company: Collectible World Studios — U.K.
Parent company of many lines, including Pocket Dragons,
Piggin', Eyes for You, and more.
Site Features: Info on catalogue • Join collectors' clubs
• Online shopping some items • Message board

COUNTRY ARTISTS
http://www.countryartists.com/
Company: Country Artists — U.K.
Creators of upscale, highly detailed wildlife sculptures. Hand-
made and handpainted in Stratford-on-Avon. Probably the
best in this type of line. The Web site doubles as the American
distributor.
Site Features: Info on current catalogue and various lines
• Company history

DAVID WINTER
http://www.enesco.com
Company: Enesco Corp. — U.S.
Britain's David Winter is the original creator of contemporary,
miniature architectural art, and after twenty years he still does
incredible work.
Site Features: Info on current catalogue • News
• Join collectors' club online

DEPARTMENT 56
http://www.department56.com
Company: Department 56, Inc. — U.S.
Low-end architectural art that lights up. Its low price-
point makes Department 56 very popular, particularly for
Christmas displays.
Site Features: Info on current catalogue • News • Games

DISCWORLD
http://www.clarecraft.com
Company: Clarecraft — U.K.
Figurines based on the fantasy novels of Terry Pratchett. A wonderfully cheeky site run by the hilarious, self-deprecating Elton.
Site Features: Info on complete catalogue • News • Online shopping • Join collectors' club online

DREAMSICLES
http://www.dreamsicles.com
Company: Cast Art Industries — U.S.
Cherub figurines made of resin and hydro-stone (whatever that is).
Site Features: Info on current catalogue • Join collectors' club • "Members-only" auction site (an excellent idea)

ENCHANTICA
http://www.enchantica.com
Company: Holland Studio Craft — U.K.
Spectacular dragon and fantasy figurines. A must for medieval maniacs.
Site Features: Info on complete catalogue • Message board • Chat room • Production process

ERTL
http://www.ertltoys.com
Company: The Ertl Co., Inc. — U.S.
Collectors in the know claim that Ertl makes the best die-cast toys on the market.
Site Features: Info on current catalogue • News • Online shopping • Message board

FONTANINI
http://www.roman.com
Company: Roman, Inc. — U.S.
The Fontanini family carries on a ninety-year tradition of creating world-famous Nativity sets. Stunning porcelain sculptures to brighten Christmases for generations to come.
Site Features: Info on current catalogue • Message board
• Chat room

FURBY
http://207.226.169.244 (I'm not kidding)
Company: Tiger Electronics — Japan
Famously annoying plush, talking electronic toy. (When at the site, I turned off the audio in case the Furbys said anything.) Slow-loading, but a great site for kids.
Site Features: Info on complete catalogue • News • Games
• Message board

GALOOB
http://www.galoob.com
Company: Galoob Toys, Inc. — U.S.
While the big boys, like Mattel, are busy chasing today's collectibles, Galoob is busy building tomorrow's — Pound Puppies, Treasure Trolls, Spice Girls, Micro Machines — apparently anything with two words in its title.
Site Features: Info on current catalogues • News • Shopping online

GENE DOLL
http://www.genedoll.com
Company: Ashton-Drake Galleries — U.S.
"Barbie" for adults. Mel Odom's nostalgic fashion doll, "Gene Marshall," is a '90s phenomenon. Designer outfits with a '40s flair will make you pine for *Casablanca.*
Site Features: Info on complete catalogue • Message board
• Chat room

G.I. JOE
http://www.gijoe.com
Company: Hasbro, Inc. — U.S.
"Barbie" for boys. Old Joe has been around since 1964, and he's got plenty of history and products to sell.
Site Features: Info on complete catalogue • News
• Shopping online

GREENWICH WORKSHOP
http://www.greenwichworkshop.com
Company: Greenwich Workshop — U.K.
Fantastical, humorous fine art and sculptures, notably by James Christensen and Will Bullas. Gorgeous site matches the classy product. Christensen's art, where the Renaissance and the surreal collide, is especially entertaining. If only I had the money.
Site Features: Info on complete catalogue

GUND
http://www.gund.com
Company: Gund, Inc. — U.S.
Century-old manufacturer of first-class stuffed teddy bears and other critters. Next to Steiff's, the best bears around.
Site Features: Info on current catalogue • News • Games

HALLMARK
http://www.hallmark.com
Company: Hallmark Cards Inc. — U.S.
Producer of top-quality ornaments and cards. Hallmark's limited edition ornaments, such as Barbie and Kiddie Car Classics, do extremely well on the secondary market. Good site.
Site Features: Info on current catalogue • Shop online • News
• Join collectors club online

HARBOUR LIGHTS
http://www.HarbourLights.com
Company: Harbour Lights — U.S.
Miniature architectural art of all manner of lighthouses. I really liked this site — it is simple and clear, with tons of information and fascinating details.
Site Features: Info on complete catalogue • News
• Join collectors' club online • Message board
• Chat room • Histories of actual lighthouses sculpted

HARMONY KINGDOM
http://www.harmonykingdom.com
Company: The Harmony Ball Co. — U.S.
Clever, hilarious, and beautiful ceramic boxes that usually depict animals up to no good.
Site Features: Info on complete catalogue • News • Join collectors' club online • Kids' play-area with puzzles • Fans will love the "secrets" behind the boxes

HASBRO
http://www.hasbro.com
or http://www.hasbrocollectors.com (The Hasbro Store)
Company: Hasbro, Inc. — U.S.
Parent company of many toys that have become collectibles, including G.I. Joe, Transformers, Starting Lineup, Tonka, etc. Fun site for kids.
Site Features: Info on current catalogue • News • Games
• The Hasbro store is great! Your wallet will be begging you to leave.

HOT WHEELS
http://www.hotwheels.com
Company: Mattel, Inc. — U.S.
Miniature die-cast cars are a very hot collectible, especially for men, and Hot Wheels are well established. Great site with lots of info on the actual full-size vehicles. But then, I'm a man...
Site Features: Info on current catalogue • News • Games • Join collectors' club online • Shopping online • Internet exclusives

JIM BEAM
http://www.jimbeam.com
Company: James B. Beam Distilling Co. — U.S.
They may make bourbon, but — as with PEZ — it's the dispenser that counts. Marvellous sculptural bottles that collectors just can't get enough of. This is an age-sensitive site that is set up like an animated bar, with a bartender and a band. Very cool!
Site Features: Info on catalogue • Music • Pool game

JUST THE RIGHT SHOE
http://www.willitts.com
Company: Willitts Designs — U.S.
Miniature resin fashion footwear with an historic bent.
Site Features: Info on complete catalogue • Message board

LILLIPUT LANE
http://www.enesco.com
Company: Enesco Corp. — U.S.
First-rate miniature masterpieces of architectural art made in the U.K. Hand-made and hand-painted, the detail on these sculptures is overwhelming. Who'd a thunk you could do this with plaster?
Site Features: Info on current catalogue • News • Join collectors' club online

LLADRO
http://www.lladro.org/indexen.html
Company: Lladro — Spain
The Rolls-Royce of figurine manufacturers. Elegant porcelain figurines with a Spanish influence. Absolutely sublime. This is *the* premier Web site for a collectible, as beautiful as the product it promotes.
Site Features: News • Info on catalogue

LONGABERGER BASKETS
http://www.longaberger.com/
Company: The Longaberger Company — U.S.
Initially started with collectible woven baskets and have expanded into home furnishings.
Site Features: News • Info on catalogue

MADAME ALEXANDER DOLLS
http://www.alexanderdoll.com
Company: The Alexander Doll Company — U.S.
Premier American doll company with long and honoured history. "Cissy" is probably their most famous creation.
Site Features: Info on catalogue • News

MARY'S MOO MOOS
http://www.enesco.com
Company: Enesco Corp. — U.S.
Resin figurines of cows at work and play. (I don't make these things up.)
Site Features: Info on catalogue • News

MATCHBOX
http://www.mattel.com/branded/matchbox
Company: Mattel, Inc. — U.S.
British line of high-quality die-cast vehicles. My mom threw all of mine out. If I'd only known . . . The site is practically useless. You're better off going to the Mattel Online store and cruising the Matchbox products there. Just follow the store link at the top of the page.
Site Features: Info on a few currents

MATS JONASSON SIGNATURE COLLECTION
http://www.matsjonasson.com
Company: Maleras Glasbruk — Sweden
Stunning crystal sculptures, primarily of wildlife, by Mats Jonasson, who also creates elegant paperweights and glassware. His colleague, Erika Hoglund, is making a name for herself with her line of sensuous female sculptures. A collectible to watch.
Site Features: Info on current catalogue

MATTEL
http://www.mattel.com
Company: Mattel, Inc. — U.S.
Parent company of many lines other than Barbie — Cabbage Patch Kids, Winnie the Pooh, Tyco, Fisher-Price, Sesame Street, Nickelodeon, Hot Wheels, and more. Unfortunately, in spite of the millions it has made from children's toys, there are no games or other kind of entertainment for kids on Mattel's site. They should take a lesson from Disney or Ty. The store, however, is amazing.
Site Features: Info on current catalogues • News • Shopping online at the Mattel Store

McDONALD'S
http://www.mcdonalds.com/mcdonaldland/whatsnew/
happy_meal/index.html
Company: McDonald's Corp. — U.S.
"Happy Meal" giveaways stretch back to 1977 and thousands
of people collect them. The site has great animation.
Site Features: Info on current giveaways • Games

MEANIES
http://www.meanies.com
Company: The Idea Factory — U.S.
Beanbag toys, created initially as a parody of Beanie Babies,
have taken on a life of their own. Site has a cloying "mock"
attitude, guaranteed to offend no one.
Site Features: Info on catalogue • Games • News

M.I. HUMMEL
http://www.mihummel.com
Company: W. Goebel Porzellanfabrik — Germany
Venerable line of porcelain figurines of children who just can't
keep their mouths shut.
Site Features: Info on current catalogue • Join collectors' club
online • Info on marks of authenticity

MOORCROFT
http://www.moorcroft.co.uk
Company: Moorcroft Ltd. — U.K.
Highly respected century-old pottery manufacturer.
Site Features: Info on current catalogue • Info on historic
company marks

MYTH & MAGIC
http://www.tudormint.com
Company: The Tudor Mint — U.S.
Fantasy pewter figurines, including a line from *Lord of the Rings*.
Site Features: Info on current catalogue

PENDELFIN
http://www.pendelfin.co.uk
Company: Pendelfin Studios Ltd. — U.K.
Hand-painted stoneware rabbits that seem to keep multiplying.
Site Features: Info on catalogue • News

PEZ
http://www.pez.com
Company: PEZ Candy, Inc. — U.S.
The innovative flip-top candy dispensers made PEZ the legend
that it is today. A disappointing site for such a colourful product.
Site Features: Info on complete catalogue • Online shopping

PIGGIN'
http://www.piggin.com/index.cgi
Company: Collectible World Studios — U.K.
Funny pig figurines at work and play created by Dave
Corbidge. Fun site!
Site Features: Info on complete catalogue • News • Shopping
online • Chat room • Games

POCKET DRAGONS
http://www.pocket-dragons.com/index.cgi
Company: Collectible World Studios — U.K.
Cute, mischievous little green dragons that have survived the
Ages by hiding in people's pockets. Created by Real Musgrave.
Site Features: Info on complete catalogue • News • Shopping
online • Chat room

POKÉMON
http://www.pokemon.com
Company: Nintendo — U.S.
The official Web site of those lovable mutants from that mysterious island. All things Pokémon are listed here. Excellent resource for Pokémaniacs.
Site Features: Info on current lines • News • Games • Links to Nintendo's online store

PRECIOUS MOMENTS
http://www.enesco.com
Company: Enesco Corp. — U.S.
Bisque figurines of doe-eyed children with a religious bent, created by Sam Butcher.
Site Features: Info on current catalogue • News
Here's another site:
http://www.preciousmoments.com
Company: Precious Moments Inc. — U.S.
Chapel for aforementioned figurines that is a disquieting mix of faith and commerce. Only in America.
Site Features: Info on complete catalogue • News • Shopping online some items • Chat room

PRETTY AS A PICTURE
http://www.enesco.com
Company: Enesco Corp. — U.S.
Bisque figurines of children dressed in oversized adult clothing, based on the work of photographer Kim Anderson.
Site Features: Info on current catalogue • News

PUFFKINS
http://www.swibco.com
Company: Swibco Inc. — U.S.
Puffy stuffed animals. Been there, done that. Good site for kids.
Site Features: Info on complete catalogue • News • Games
• Chat room • Message board

RADKO ORNAMENTS
http://www.radko.com
Company: Starad Inc. — U.S.
Elegant, mouth-blown glass ornaments, based on designs by
Christopher Radko. Terrific site that matches the quality of
the product.
Site Features: Info on current catalogue • News
• Online shopping

ROBERT TONNER DOLLS
http://www.roberttonner.com
Company: Robert Tonner Doll Company — U.S.
Vinyl and porcelain fashion dolls designed by Robert Tonner.
Site Features: Info on complete catalogue

ROYAL DOULTON
http://www.royal-doulton.co.uk
Company: Royal Doulton — U.K.
One of the world's most famous ceramics manufacturers.
Figurines, Toby jugs, tableware, the lot.
Site Features: Info on current catalogue

SERAPHIM CLASSICS
http://www.roman.com
Company: Roman, Inc. — U.S.
Resin, pastel-shaded angels.
Site Features: Info on complete catalogue • Message board
• Chat room • Games

SMURFS
http://www.smurf.com
Company: Studio Peyo — Switzerland / IMPS — Belgium
Believe it or not, these little blue critters have been around for more than forty years! I have new-found respect. Good site.
Site Features: Info on current catalogue • Games
• Shopping online

STAR WARS
http://www.starwars.com
Company: Lucasfilms Ltd. — U.S.
All things Star Wars, and there's plenty of them. This is *the* state-of-the-art Web site. You can spend lots of time, and lots of money, here. Spectacular!
Site Features: Info on the complete movie series • Games
• News • Shopping online • Film clips

STARTING LINEUP
http://www.startinglineup.com
Company: Hasbro, Inc. — U.S.
Sports fans love this line of figures of famous athletes. Super site with lots of info.
Site Features: Info on current catalogue • News • Join collectors' club online • Shopping in Hasbro's store online
• Games • Sports trivia

STEIFF
http://www.steiff.com or http://www.steiffusa.com
Company: Margarete Steiff GmbH — Germany
Probably the most respected teddy bear manufacturer in the world.
Site Features: Info on current catalogue • News
• Exchange board

SWAROVSKI
http://www.swarovski.com
Company: Swarovski AG — Austria
Century-old manufacturer of exquisite crystal collectibles.
Swarovski figurines have always been appreciated on the
secondary market, making them a great investment.
Elegant site.
Site Features: Info on current catalogue • News

TENDER TAILS
http://www.enesco.com/misc/tndrtail/thome.htm
Company: Enesco Corp. — U.S.
Plush animals from the folks who brought you Precious
Moments. Best viewed on Gravol.
Site Features: Info on complete catalogue • News

UNIVERSAL STUDIOS
http://www.universalstudios.com
Company: Universal Studios — U.S.
Company store has film products for sale, both nostalgic
and current.
Site Features: Info on current catalogue • News on new
movies • Online shopping

WADE
http://www.wade.co.uk/homef.htm
Company: Wade Ceramics Ltd. — U.K.
All manner of ceramic products from almost 200 years of
manufacturing, notably fairy-tale figurines.
Site Features: Info on current catalogue • Join collectors' club
online • "Members-only" shopping online

WALT DISNEY CLASSICS
http://disney.go.com
Company: Disney — U.S.
You know you've really made it when they drop the "www"
from your URL. Masterful porcelain sculptures based on
Disney characters. Unfortunately, there's so much on this site
that it's a bit confusing.
Site Features: Amazing animation (of course!) • Info on cur-
rent Disney products • Games • Online shopping • News
• Much more

WARNER BROTHERS
http://www.wbstore.com
Company: Warner Bros. — U.S.
Bugs Bunny, Batman, Pokémon, Wile E. Coyote — products
featuring the whole Warners gang (including those fabulous
"Looney Tunes" porcelain sculptures from Goebel) are up
for sale.
Site Features: Info on current catalogue • News
• Shopping online

WEDGWOOD
http://www.wedgwood.co.uk
Company: Wedgwood — U.K.
Jasper ware and other fine china from the renowned
Wedgwood.
Site Features: Info on current catalogue • Join collectors' club
online (U.K. residents only) • Shopping online

WIZARDS & DRAGONS
http://www.wizards-dragons.com/index.cgi
Company: Collectible World Studios — U.K.
Brilliant fantasy sculptures by the inimitable Hap Henriksen.
Site Features: Info on complete catalogue

SITES FOR SORE EYES

Here is my "Top Ten" list, chosen based on technical and artistic prowess, ease of navigation, sense of fun, and/or because they do justice to the quality of their collectible.

1. Star Wars
2. Lladro
3. Coca-Cola
4. Jim Beam
5. Radko Ornaments
6. Furby
7. Harbour Lights
8. Caithness Glass
9. Cardew Design
10. Hot Wheels

Collectibles Companies Without Web Sites

COLOUR BOX
Resin cat and bear figurines made in Scotland.

HAGEN-RENAKER
Miniature animal figurines.

KRYSTONIA
Ceramic dragons, wizards, fantasy figures. Although this line has been around for a long time, I couldn't find a company Web site.

SCHMID
Manufacturer of highly collectible, licensed, ceramic music boxes — Ended production in 1995. No site found. This is a rising star among collectibles.

APPENDIX 2

Cruising Some Auction Sites

THERE ARE HUNDREDS, if not thousands, of auction sites on the Internet. I've highlighted a few of the biggest in Part II of this book, and brief descriptions of those, along with many more, are included here (in no particular order). These are all real-time auctions.

EBAY
www.ebay.com
This site is so popular that when it goes down — and it does, frequently — it's actually covered on the evening news. In spite of its many drawbacks, it is undeniably the best site for buying and selling collectibles, mainly because of the volume of traffic. It's easy to dislike the front-runner, but eBay is making a real effort to be cordial to its customers. My one quibble is that they charge a fee to set a reserve price.

AUCTIONS.COM
www.auctions.com
Formerly Auction Universe, this site should be the giant on the Net. There are no listing fees, and the commission is a straight-forward 2.5 percent across the board. The site has had a tough time grabbing business from the leader, but that should change

as more buyers become frustrated with eBay's downtime, and perhaps as they become familiar with the easier-to-remember Web address.

UP4SALE
www.up4sale.com/
A subsidiary of eBay, Up4Sale is free — no listing fees and no commissions, although it does charge for such optional bells and whistles as boldface listings. It's a great "garage sale" site for low-end items, but not particularly useful for buying and selling anything upscale. You won't be bidding on a Rolls Royce Silver Cloud here.

THE SERIOUS COLLECTOR
www.seriouscollector.com/
A hybrid between a mall and an auction site, The Serious Collector is an idea whose time has come — a site that deals primarily in high-end items and collectibles. In spite of its pretensions, the listing fees are reasonable and the extended auctions are a plus for sellers. A simple, clean site — one of my faves.

AMAZON.COM AUCTIONS
www.amazon.com/auctions
Essentially a clone of eBay. At least they don't charge you for using a reserve.

YAHOO! AUCTIONS
auctions.yahoo.com/
Like Up4Sale, Yahoo! auctions are free. They have the interesting feature of allowing sellers to predetermine either a fixed or flexible closing time for their auctions. Oddly, the Yahoo! staff determines which items will be "featured auctions."

EHAMMER
www.ehammer.com

ehammer seems to deal mostly in antiques and Americana. They have a section for classified ads, as well as real-time auctions with extended time during the last ninety seconds. One unique feature is the "auction hall": sellers can rent their own virtual auction hall for thirty days for a fee of $175. In your hall, only your own items are listed. An ideal way to eliminate the competition.

AUCTION ADVENTURES
www.auctionadventures.net

This site looks like someone made it in their basement. If you care to try it out, the listings are free, and they only charge a one percent commission on completed sales. Maybe they should raise the commission and hire a designer.

GOLD'S AUCTION
www.goldsauction.com/

Another eBay clone. Quite a substantial site, with lots of items listed when I visited. The fee structure is similar to eBay, as is the look. Has potential.

GOODWILL AUCTIONS
www.shopgoodwill.com/

Bad news for collectors, but great news for charities — Goodwill has finally realized what a gold mine its donations are! (No more bargains down at the local outlet, I'm afraid.) Their site, which is supported by 182 Goodwill outlets throughout the U.S. and Canada, offers up donated items from their vast inventory. Bidding was hot and heavy when I dropped by, and all the proceeds go to charity. The site was clean and simple to navigate. Great idea!

BIDMORE
www.bidmore.com

A young upstart that doesn't charge fees. Extended time on auctions if there's a bid in the last five minutes. Nothing special.

ARCTICAUCTION
www.arcticauction.com/

A perfect example of a bad auction site. Very slow to load, messy graphics, illegible colours, lots of categories with nothing in them. Other than the cool name, I have nothing good to say about this site.

AUCTIONFLOOR
www.auctionfloor.com/

Computer Disk Service Corporation specializes in hard drives, and they seem to have set up this auction site primarily to feature electronics and computer-related auctions. There are no listing fees, but sellers pay a commission on items sold. There was wind whistling through the empty categories when I came calling.

BID.COM
www.bid.com

Wow, what a mess! This combination mall and auction site started in Canada, and has spread its tentacles across the Net. It seems to be dominated by electronics and computer-related items. Canadians can shop in Canadian dollars, Americans in U.S. dollars, and so on. It has an interesting feature called a "declining Dutch Auction": as the auction progresses, the price continually drops until all the duplicates have been sold. Good for buyers, bad for sellers. Navigation was completely baffling, loading time was slow, graphics were unappealing, and it had ad banners on every single page. (One of my pet peeves on auction sites, as if they are not making enough money!) It looked like there were some pretty good deals on computers, though…

BID2BID
www.bid2bid.com
Another miserable, slow-loading site, a combination of a whole-sale shopping mall and auction. Terrible graphics and confusing navigation. Its main distinction is that every auction starts at one cent and there are no reserves. Presumably listings are free, but I couldn't find the info on that. This site is so slow, they should pay you to sit there.

EXCITE AUCTIONS
auctions.excite.com
The owners of the popular portal/search engine have opened their own auction site, and it seemed to be dominated by elec-tronic items. It's a good, clean site that is easy to navigate. List-ings are free, and there is a commission on items that are sold. One feature I liked was a real-time clock on the individual item pages where you can see those precious bidding seconds count-ing down. What I hated — the usual: ad banners!

GLOBAL AUCTION ONLINE!
www.global-auction.com
I had two concerns when I hit this one — there was an ad ban-ner for eBay (hey, guys, aren't they your competition?) and the "Auction Fees" section was "under construction." Hmmm. At the moment, listings are free with the usual accoutrement of enhancements for a fee. Again, I heard the sound of wind whistling.

iTRADE
www.itrade.com

Was ist iTrade? It's a gorgeous German auction site, proving once again that no one understands design better than the Europeans. Unfortunately, the entire site is in German and the prices are in deutsche marks. I'm afraid my five years of Latin did not prepare me for translating German. Couldn't follow what was going on, but the site looked quite busy. Hey, when's somebody going to start a site in Latin?

JEWELNET AUCTIONS
www.jewelnetauctions.com

This site is selling mainly — guess what? — jewellery. I quite liked this one. Very clean and simple, and I loved the font in the titles. I really appreciated the info they provided right up front on the home page under the opening title: "NO LISTING FEES 1% Commission fee charged only if your item sells." Why can't they all be that straightforward? Although Jewelnet had some other items listed — such as Oriental rugs — I would recommend this as the spot to buy and sell your baubles.

LYCOS AUCTIONS
auctions.lycos.com/

Another search engine with an auction to grind. Smartly laid out and easy to navigate. No listing fees. No commissions. No customers. There were plenty of items listed for auction, but very few of them had any bids. If you're a bargain hunter, this would be a good site to keep an eye on.

EDEAL AUCTIONS
www.edeal.com

Just when you think you can't bear to look at another mediocre auction site, along comes edeal. This is the epitome of a well laid out auction site. Beautiful, quick-loading graphics and clearly marked categories and instructions. There are no listing fees, but sellers are charged commissions similar to those on eBay. They have their own in-house escrow service and a "Fraud Busters" program — the site contacts the proper authorities in case of fraud. As far as I know, no other auction site takes a lick of interest in saving its patrons from being fleeced. edeal also has an "ipoints" program, whereby you can collect points by buying and selling, and redeem them for prizes later. Lots of items were listed, but bidding was slow to non-existent. Too bad. The folks who made edeal got it right, and they should be rewarded for it. I know I'm going to start using this site.

MSN AUCTIONS
auctions.msn.com

The first item I saw up for bid when I arrived was "Buy A College Degree — Legally!" — and who would know more about the law than Microsoft, who seem to be spending a considerable amount of money and time in courtrooms as of late. Perhaps they can devote more attention to their auction site in the near future. It's a run-of-the-mill site whose only remarkable feature was that it has exactly the same program and layout as Lycos Auctions — only the headers are different. I guess Bill owns that, too. Listings are free, sellers pay a commission. Now that I have a degree, I will figure out the fee structure and get back to you.

NETSHOPPERS.COM
www.netshoppers.com

Free, free, free! Nothing here, here, here. And their logo looks like an eBay rip-off.

ONLINEAUCTIONS
www.onlineauctions.com

Nicely made site with some interesting features. Sellers can download a program that enables them to write multiple listings offline and post them all with one command. Among its various auction formats is one called "Penny Over." When you bid one cent over the opening bid, you win the auction. Sort of curtails the thrill a bit, doesn't it? Sellers pay a listing fee, and the commission on sales is 2.5 percent, no matter how much the item sells for. Don't sell your "Superman #1" here. The site was relatively busy when I dropped by, so the gang has discovered it.

THEBARGAINHUT
www.TheBargainHut.com

They promote themselves as "The Home of the FirstBidWins." In other words, the first person who bids the opening price wins the auction. (Where I come from, they call this practice "buying something," not "winning an auction.") TheBargainHut also offers sellers a choice of two fee schemes: if you pay a listing fee up front, you won't be charged a commission when the item sells; on the other hand you can skip the listing fee and pay a 4 percent commission when you sell. Slightly messy site and navigation was not clearly marked. Plus, it had ad banners.

TINY AUCTIONS
www.tinyauctions.co.uk

As you can tell by the URL, this auction site is based in England, and "tiny" does not refer to the items up for sale — it's the name of the British computer manufacturer that owns the site. Prices are in pounds sterling, and the seller's fee is a 3 percent commission on sales. Good, clean site with clear navigation. Business was a tad slack when I dropped by.

MY TOP TEN PICKS

1. edeal
2. The Serious Collector
3. eBay
4. auctions.com
5. Goodwill Auctions
6. Gold's Auction
7. iTrade
8. Jewelnet
9. OnLine Auctions
10. Tiny Auctions

Web Sites Cited in This Book

Gulliver's Collectibles	www.gulliverscollectibles.com
Add Me	www.add-me.com
Advanced Book Exchange	www.abebooks.com
Angelfire	www.angelfire.com
Another Universe	www.AnotherUniverse.com
Collectible-Info	www.collectible-info.com
Collectibles Exchange	www.colexch.com
Collectors Net	www.collectorsnet.com
Collectors Online	www.collectorsonline.com
Collectors Web	www.collectorsweb.com
Curioscape	www.curioscape.com
Geocities	www.geocities.com
Library of Congress	http://rs6.loc.gov/amhome.html
OHI Exchange	www.ohiexchange.com
Swappers and Collectors	www.swappersandcollectors.com
White's Guide	www.whitesguide.com
World Collectors Net	www.worldcollectorsnet.com
Yahoo!	www.yahoo.com

Index